4/22/95
For my dear friends,
Max + Edith
Bud Milder

Advance Praise for

THE GOOD BOOK SAYS . . .

Milder tweaks the Bible and titillates the reader with a gentle cynicism and lilting, humorous rhymes. This is, in itself, a good book.

— Dick Emmons, author of *Having a Wonderful Rhyme, Wish You Were Here*

A clever concept, wittily executed.

— Robert N. Feinstein, author of *Son of an Oyster* and *Oyster's Last Stand*

Through prophets and proverbs, inceptions and law,
These verses will lead you like another Esau —
With wisdom and wit and in lines so fine,
Your tongue will dance down every line.

— William Gass, author of *The Habitations of the Word*

Biblical exegesis may seem an unlikely source of smiles, but Ben Milder's deft verse succeeds both in keeping us entertained and in casting new light on the Old Testament. Doubting Thomases might sample, for a start, "The Garden of Eden, No Club Med," "Sodom Chloride," and "The Sacrifice of Isaac" — accounts that startlingly differ from the ones we heard in Sunday School. *The Good Book Says . . .* is guaranteed to cheer you up the next time you find yourself in a hotel room with only a Gideon Bible and a broken TV set, and your room-service breakfast is an hour late.

— X.J. Kennedy, author of *Cross Ties: Selected Poems*

Dr. Milder has not only illumined but enlivened the Old Testament with his witty and ingeniously rhymed verses. Daily readings from this book in schools might well be preferable to the proposed daily moment of silence.

— Felicia Lamport, author of *Light Metres* and *Scrap Irony*

Ben Milder's *The Good Book Says . . .: Light Verse to Illuminate the Old Testament* is a humorous retelling in verse of some of the most important episodes of the Old Testament. In every instance Dr. Milder captures the heart of the episode and recasts it in a delightfully humorous mode which teases us into looking at the scriptural events in a fresh way. The humor humanizes the divine. What the author has done here reminds me of the humor that pervades some of the medieval miracle or mystery plays and the drolleries that appear in the border decorations of some medieval illuminated manuscripts. The reader of these poems is in for some very wholesome and hearty laughs.

— M.B. McNamee, S.J.

There's an honored tradition which goes back (at least) to the early eighteenth century, when Pope cast his immortal mock-heroic couplets about a woman's cosmetics. If Pope can talk "seriously" of light matters, Ben Milder, reversing the tradition, sings lightly of deep matters: Job, and the Book of Psalms, and Genesis, where it all began . . . with such wonderful couplets as the one describing Noah, after the Flood:

He sent a dove, which signaled "fini"
And brought back olives for his martini.

Or this, on Lot's wife:

. . . and when
Her curiosity subsided,
Lot found her — sodium chlorided!

which concludes,

Now, this tale should not be read with malice
But, just possibly, cum grano salis.

Or, on Jonah and his cetacean:

He just said, "Moby, open wide,"
And, presto, Jonah was inside, . . .

Such levity may strike some as inappropriate. But it embodies a well-worn aesthetic truth, that incongruities and differences are what make a poem (or any other work of art for that matter) hum, and give off energy. This is the source of Dr. Milder's very funny poems. For anyone even remotely versed in the Bible, they're a pleasure to read. And for those agnostics among us (for whom the Bible should, at any rate, be a cultural artifact), they're a pleasurable Bible Study Class — without the tedium.

Milder on Ruth ("Whither thou goest, I will go"):

"Where thy head rests, I'll put mine.
When thou borrowest, I'll cosign.
Whatever course you may pursue,
I'll stick to you like Elmer's glue."

Read — and hear a new ring to some old verses.

— John Mella, Editor, *Light: The Quarterly of Light Verse*

As a faithful reader of the Holy Book and with deep respect for the divine authority, Dr. Ben Milder has the literary skill and the courage to reproduce Biblical myths and legends in deliberately diversified, but clearly entertaining, poetic form.

The product inevitably does two things to the reader: (1) it gives one a new light upon the meaning of the original text, in a clear and insightful way; (2) in a twist of words and context, with prophetic insight, it makes the text speak in critical, and even with disparaging, emphasis, but always in a jovial way, to some modern situation and present-day issue of life.

It is a lot of fun, and it challenges the reader to put one's faith where it belongs!

— Allen O. Miller, Emeritus Professor of Systematic
Theology and Philosophy, Eden Theological Seminary

The Good Book Says . . .

Light Verse to Illuminate the Old Testament

The Good Book Says . . .

Light Verse to Illuminate the Old Testament

by

Ben Milder

TIME BEING BOOKS®
POETRY IN SIGHT AND SOUND

Time Being Books®
10411 Clayton Road
St. Louis, Missouri 63131

Time Being Books® is an imprint of Time Being Press®
Saint Louis, Missouri

Time Being Press® is a 501(c)(3) not-for-profit corporation.

Time Being Books® volumes are printed on acid-free paper, and binding materials are chosen for strength and durability.

Library of Congress Cataloging-in-Publication Data:

Milder, Benjamin, 1915-
The Good Book says — : light verse to illuminate the Old Testament / by Ben Milder. — 1st ed.
p. cm.
ISBN 1-56809-013-7. — ISBN 1-56809-014-5 (pbk.)
1. Bible. O.T. — History of Biblical events — Poetry. 2. Religious poetry, American. 3. Humorous poetry, American. I. Title.
PS3563.I37159G66 1995
811'.54 — dc20

95-5159
CIP

Cover and illustrations by *Amour Krupnick*
Book design and typesetting by *Lori Loesche*
Manufactured in the United States of America

First Edition, first printing (June 1995)

Acknowledgments

I have discovered that, without a team of expert guides, a writer could well become lost on the road from pen and paper to a published book. It gives me great pleasure to express my thanks and appreciation to my guide team at Time Being Books: Jerry Call, Editor in Chief, Lori Loesche, Editor, and Sheri Vandermolen, Editor. Their advice and untiring efforts have been invaluable in bringing this book to fruition.

I am also indebted to the cadre of clergy who gave freely of their wisdom and counsel — the ministers, rabbis, and priests who have encouraged me in this endeavor.

The following sources were used for the purposes of this book and are indicated in parentheses following each italicized passage:

(1) The Holy Bible — Revised Standard Version (New York: Thomas Nelson & Sons, 1952).

(2) The Holy Scriptures According to the Masoretic Text (Philadelphia: The Jewish Publication Society of America, 1917).

(3) The Writings-Kethubim — A New Translation of The Holy Scriptures According to the Masoretic Text (Philadelphia: The Jewish Publication Society of America, 1982).

for Jeanne

Contents

The Writings

The Good Book Says . . .

Light Verse to Illuminate the Old Testament

Reinhold Niebuhr says that the essence of sin is to take ourselves too seriously. There is something fundamentally righteous and holy about our humor.

— William H. Willimon, *And the Laugh Shall Be First: A Treasury of Religious Humor*

Pre-face

An endless crew of nameless sages
Has tampered with the Bible's pages
And managed to make rearrangeable
A text that many thought unchangeable.

That the Good Book's somewhat short on humor
Is more than just an idle rumor,
And though there are no criticisms
Of the paucity of witticisms,
The Bible's awfully gloom-and-doomerous,
And most folks do not find it humorous,

Yet, in the Bible, you will find,
Just as did the undersigned,
Leviticus has levity,
In Proverbs, wit and brevity.
There's laughter found in Genesis
And King Saul's clumsy menaces.

Therefore, with whimsical intent,
This volume's meant to supplement
Those ancient sages of this planet
Who thought their words were cast in granite.
Within these covers, you'll get word of
Details that they had not heard of.

If this enlightened disquisition
Departs a little from tradition,
It should be clear that it's not meant
To be one bit irreverent,
And should its message seem unique,
Remember this: it's "tongue in cheek."

— Ben Milder

The Law

Genesis 2:1-2

[1]And the heaven and the earth were finished, and all the host of them. [2]And on the seventh day God finished His work which He had made; and He rested on the seventh day from all His work which He had made. (2)

In the Big Inning

The Good Book says, though it's debated,
That the world we live in was created
In six short days — God didn't shirk.
On the seventh, He was out of work!
And the Good Book gives no explanation
Of how He managed that creation.

Although some circles academic
Engage, at times, in a polemic
Devoted to the proposition
That the world was formed by nuclear fission,
Most clergymen, you'll note, are leery
Of swallowing that "big bang" theory . . .

'Cause what the Good Book says prevails,
And it needn't fuss about details!

Genesis 3:1, 6-7

[1]Now the serpent was more subtle than any beast of the field . . .

[6]And when the woman saw that the tree . . . was to be desired to make one wise, she took of the fruit thereof, and did eat; and she gave also unto her husband with her, and he did eat; . . .
[7]And the eyes of them both were opened, and they knew that they were naked; . . . (2)

The Garden of Eden, No Club Med

The Good Book says that Adam,
Along with Eve, his madam,
Were happy with the life that they were leadin'.
Since the nearest nudist beach
Was most likely out of reach,
They simply ran around unclad in Eden

Till the serpent, who was sinister,
Proceeded to administer
A sample of the Lord's forbidden fruit,
Which at once made them aware
That they were completely bare,
Arrayed in what we'd call their "birthday suit."

And because of that mean asp,
Eve and Adam came to grasp
Just why the tree of knowledge was forbidden,
And they made a dash, posthaste,
To be clad below the waist
So their private parts, so called, would be well hidden.

Those were serious offenses
With long-lasting consequences —
Because they sinned, today there's no escape.
Bad enough that we have clothes,
But the fashions they impose
Are meant to keep us all bent out of shape.

Every female now must suffer
Garments into which they stuff 'er —
Such things as girdles, bras and pantyhose —
Men wear ties that tend to choke 'em,
Jockey shorts that seem to poke 'em —
And what they'll think of next, God only knows.

~ Lesson ~

If a snake appears one night,
Says, "Here's an apple, have a bite,"
Remember what, in Genesis, you've read.
Though he promises an Eden,
If you have done your readin'
You probably would settle for Club Med!

Genesis 4:8-9

[8]And Cain spoke unto Abel his brother. And it came to pass, when they were in the field, that Cain rose up against Abel his brother, and slew him. [9]And the Lord said unto Cain: 'Where is Abel thy brother?' And he said: 'I know not; am I my brother's keeper?' (2)

Raising Cain

Two children graced the Adams' table
Before Cain went and slaughtered Abel.
One thing, it seems, led to another;
The Lord said, "Cain, where is your brother?"

"Am I my brother's keeper?" said he.
The Lord replied, "Enough already —
We both know what you've done is horrid,"
And He placed a mark upon Cain's forehead.

Since hanging was not yet in fashion,
The Good Lord acted with compassion:
Banished . . . but Cain served no time
For what seems like a heinous crime.

Though, in this topsy-turvy century,
Some crooks escape the penitentiary,
No news today could be absurder
Than how Cain got away with murder,

But Cain was spared that one-way journey,
So he must have had a good attorney.

Genesis 4:17

[17]And Cain knew his wife; and she conceived,
and bore Enoch; . . . (2)

Mrs. Cain, Nee?

In Genesis, we're in the middle
Of a hitherto unanswered riddle,
Which scholars to this very date debate.
The Good Book says Cain had a mate,
But no one knows just whence she came —
She doesn't even have a name —

And before her, there were only four of them;
Just count them up; there were no more of them.
Adam, Eve and Cain and Abel
Were all that sat around the table,
And the Bible says there's but one house,
So where did Cain dig up his spouse?

But we won't incur the Good Book's wrath,
Even though it's weak on math.

Genesis 6:14-15, 8:11

[14]Make thee an ark of gopher wood; . . . [15]And this is how thou shalt make it: the length of the ark three hundred cubits, the breadth of it fifty cubits, and the height of it thirty cubits.

[11]And the dove came in to him at eventide; and lo in her mouth an olive-leaf freshly plucked; . . . (2)

Said Noah: "What's a Cubit?"

It began in Noah's habitat
And wound up on Mount Ararat.

When the Lord saw people misbehaving,
He said, "That world just ain't worth saving.
Noah, you'd better build an ark,"
And Noah heeded that remark.

He called his sons and said, "Get going,
Because we have no way of knowing
How fast a flood will inundate us,
So let's build that floating apparatus."

They plunged in with religious fervor,
Though it was plain to an observer
Their prospects for success were dismal
'Cause their lack of knowledge was abysmal.

"At building ships I'm just a novice,"
Said Noah, "and with thousands of us,
How big an 'ark'? Is that a boat?
Can I be certain it will float?"

The Lord said, "Noah, I'll decide
How many cubits long and wide."
Moaned Noah, "Maybe we're just stupid;
Not one of us knows what's a 'cubit.'"

But the ark was built. The storm clouds blew,
And up the gangplank, two by two,
Went the beasts with Noah and his clan,
According to the Good Lord's plan.

Forty days and nights, then Noah needed
To see if the waters had receded.
Now if you were in that situation,
You'd likely glean that information

By looking starboard or to port,
But he did nothing of the sort.
He sent a dove, which signaled "*fini*"
And brought back olives for his martini.

All that rain — hard to conceive it,
But it's in the Book, so you'd best believe it!

Genesis 19:24-26

[24]Then the Lord caused to rain upon Sodom and upon Gomorrah brimstone and fire from the Lord out of heaven; [25]and He overthrew those cities, and all the Plain, and all the inhabitants of the cities, . . . [26]But his wife looked back from behind him, and she became a pillar of salt. (2)

Sodom Chloride

The Good Book says, regarding Lot,
His wife deserved just what she got
'Cause the Good Lord said to them, "Tomorra,
I'm gonna burn down Sodom and Gomorrah.
Just leave — don't look behind again,"
But she was curious, and when
Her curiousity subsided,
Lot found her — sodium chlorided!

Now, this tale should not be read with malice
But, just possibly, *cum grano salis.**

*With a grain of salt.

Genesis 21:5-6

[5]And Abraham was a hundred years old, when his son Isaac was born unto him. [6]And Sarah said: 'God hath made laughter for me; every one that heareth will laugh on account of me.' (2)

Abraham and Sarah, Parents? It's Laughable

The Good Book says, anent fertility,
That Abraham had that ability
But not before he'd made provision
To undergo a circumcision
At ninety-nine, the Bible stated —
And that's how it's authenticated.

This newly trimmed nonagenarian
Was not a man to do much tarryin'.
When Sarah smiled, his nostrils quivered:
Within one year, she had delivered
Amidst much joy and celebrating,
With the entire town participating,

And there was laughter — the Lord ordained it.
Though some have tried, no one's explained it.
Which brings to mind a modern parable
That seems to be uniquely "Sarah-able,"
A tale that may be short on verities
But has, you'll see, some similarities:

An aged man, but newly wed,
Led his nubile wife to bed.
Imagine, if you can, his joy
When she had a bouncing baby boy.

The old man now had one obsession:
Several more in quick succession.
"God bless you, doc," he said, and then,
"D'you think that I can do it again?"

The doctor laughed, let out a roar:
"What makes you think you did it before?"

Though you may scoff at this analogy
Regarding Isaac's genealogy,
The Good Book leaves us with a dearth
Of facts regarding Sarah's mirth,
And opinions are diverse and various
'Bout what her neighbors found hilarious.

→

Since questions linger, I presume,
About who was laughing, and at whom,
This chapter, in its jubilation,
Reveals a knack for obfuscation.

Genesis 22:2

[2]And He said: 'Take now thy son, thine only son, whom thou lovest, even Isaac, and get thee into the land of Moriah; and offer him there for a burnt-offering upon one of the mountains which I will tell thee of.' (2)

The Sacrifice of Isaac

The Lord told Abe it would be nice
To use Isaac as a sacrifice,
But his son was spared that one-way ticket
By a ram the Lord placed in a thicket,

And Abe's hand shook as he was proffering
The ram, instead, as a burnt offering,
For the Lord had used that whole commotion
As a test of Abraham's devotion.

Though, in Isaac's case, God intervenes,
Let's suppose your kids are in their teens,
And you've been tempted, on occasion,
To use that method of persuasion.

Resist the urge, for it's suggested
That you, like Abe, are being tested —
Not by the Lord, you should take note,
But by your kids, who get your goat.

Genesis 41:1-2

[1]And it came to pass at the end of two full years, that Pharaoh dreamed: . . . [2]And, behold, there came up out of the river seven kine, well-favoured and fat-fleshed; . . . (2)

Joseph Has a Kine Word for Pharaoh

From the Good Book's pages, we're divining
That all clouds have a silver lining,
And, in this context, they report
That while he lived in Pharaoh's court,
Young Joseph had a knack, it seems,
For understanding people's dreams.

When Pharaoh woke up one night screaming
About a strange dream he'd been dreaming,
He called on Joe, in his confusion,
To shed some light on his illusion:

Seven kine* were fat, and seven lean;
Seven ears were ripe, and seven green.
When Pharaoh called Joe to examine
That dream, Joe said, "There'll be a famine,
'Cause the fat kine ate the lean kine first
(Or perhaps I have it just reversed)."

At any rate, it sounded sinister,
So the king made Joseph his prime minister,
And the dreaded famine was averted
By the efforts Joseph had exerted.

You'd best think twice ere you assail
That story as a fairy tale,
For the Good Book's verses spell it out
That Joseph wielded all that clout!

---

*Kine:

A word that you may not have heard
Or, if you have, perhaps inferred
That kine are some exotic beast
Indigenous to the Middle East.
Though the word "kine" went out with the bustle,
They're what cattle rustlers used to rustle.

Genesis 41:47-49

[47]And in the seven years of plenty the earth brought forth in heaps. [48]And he gathered up all the food of the seven years which were in the land of Egypt, and laid up the food in the cities; the food of the field, which was round about every city, laid he up in the same. [49]And Joseph laid up corn as the sand of the sea, very much, until they left off numbering; for it was without number. (2)

The Burger King

When Joseph saved them from starvation,
Egyptians held a celebration.
They took a kine and sacrificed it.
The flesh thereof, they hacked and diced it,
Then added spices, herbs and scallions
And fashioned countless kine medallions,
Which underwent kine immolation
In gratitude for their salvation.

Now, Pharaoh didn't mind confessing
That this concoction had his blessing,
For loud hosannas could be heard
Throughout the land of Ramses III,
And still today, encomia ring
Of him they call their Burger King.

In Genesis, though well-intentioned,
Hamburgers are never mentioned,
But if hamburgers were thus invented,
Egyptians should be complimented.

Exodus 3:2

[2]And the angel of the Lord appeared to him in a flame of fire out of the midst of a bush; and he looked, and lo, the bush was burning, yet it was not consumed. (1)

The Burning Bush

Zippora, Moses' wife, was wishin'
He had a nine-to-five position.
The life they led was rather frugal,
So, in the *Midian Daily Bugle*,
She tracked down, through the want-ad pages,
A job with hoped-for better wages.

Off he went to the number listed.
Alas, no edifice existed.
Instead, a bramble bush aflame
Called out to him by his first name,
And Moses saw, with spontaneity,
That his new Boss would be the Deity.

The job the Good Lord was proposin'
Was to free the people He had chosen.
The Lord, of course, avoided mention
Of wages, hours or a pension,
Of how the sick-leave program works
Or any of the usual "perks."

The Lord said, "Live a life of purity,
And I will see to your security.
You'll keep the peace, be tax collector;
You'll be the guide and tour director."
Said Moses, "Do I have a choice?"
"You've just been drafted," said the Voice.

The Good Book says it happened thus
That Moses led the Exodus.

Exodus 4:2-3

[2]The Lord said to him, "What is that in your hand?" He said, "A rod." [3]And He said, "Cast it on the ground." So he cast it on the ground, and it became a serpent; and Moses fled from it. (1)

Can the Leper Change Its Spots?

At the burning bush, no words were minced,
But Moses still was not convinced
The people would buy, a priori,
His leadership from such a story.

The Lord said, "I think you'll persuade 'em.
You won't need an ultimatum;
I'm sure that you'll get their attention
With miracles of My invention.

"Throw down your staff, which I will make
Into a living, wriggling snake."
Moses took one look, turned green.
"That's how You plan to intervene?"

The Lord said, "That's one little sample.
I'll let you see one more example
Which ought to make a real impression.
I'll use a leper in this session —

"This should amaze 'em and confuse 'em.
Now place your hand upon your bosom."
The hand turned white and cadaverical,
And Moses promptly turned hysterical.

"Okay, Lord, that one's too scary!
I will be your emissary."
The Good Book says that's what was needed
(Though the bounds of good taste were exceeded).

However, faith must be empirical
About that very sort of miracle.

Exodus 15:19

[19]For when the horses of Pharaoh with his chariots and his horsemen went into the sea, the Lord brought back the waters of the sea upon them; but the people of Israel walked on dry ground in the midst of the sea. (1)

Parting of the Red Sea — How'd They Do That?

The Good Book says the Israelites
In Egypt had no civil rights.
They took no part in politics;
From dawn to dusk, they just made bricks.

So Moses unto Pharaoh stated,
"My people feel so alienated,"
And he vowed to even up the score
With an awful plague — and what is more,
He had nine others up his sleeve
If they did not let his people leave.

So Moses took his little band
And set out for the Promised Land.
Before them lay the deep Red Sea;
Behind them, Pharaoh's cavalry.
But Moses waved his staff and started
Across that sea, which simply parted!

How did they do that miracle,
Both Moses and C.B. De Mille?
What's more, I find it interestin',
It was also done by Charlton Heston!

But it definitely happened thus
'Cause it's there, in print, in Exodus.

Exodus 24:12, 25:2-3, 26:31-32

[12]The Lord said to Moses, "Come up to me on the mountain, and wait there; and I will give you the tables of stone, with the law and the commandment, which I have written for their instruction." (1)

[2] . . . of every man whose heart maketh him willing ye shall take My offering. [3]And this is the offering which ye shall take of them: gold, and silver, and brass; . . . (2)

[31]"And you shall make a veil of blue and purple and scarlet stuff . . . [32]and you shall hang it upon four pillars of acacia overlaid with gold, with hooks of gold, . . ." (1)

Said Moses: "They're Free? I'll Take Ten."

The Lord said, on Mount Sinai,
"I've set forth laws you must live by,"
And Moses asked, atop that mount,
"What does one cost, with my discount?"
The Lord replied, "They're free," and then
Moses answered, "I'll take ten!"

So he took the laws from the Creator
And said, "So long, Lord, I'll see you later."
But the Lord said, "Wait, I've one condition —
It's a simple work which I'll commission —
A tabernacle quite exclusive,
Something neat and unobtrusive."

For forty days, the Book discloses,
The Good Lord spelled it out for Moses
And instructed him in how to tackle
Each detail of His Tabernacle,
Including blueprints and assignments
For gold, and only gold, refinements,

Plus curtains blue and violaceous . . .
But nothing really ostentatious.
And who would pay for that creation?
Members of the congregation!
The same back then as it is today:
If you want to pray, you gotta pay!

If the Good Book says it, it's correct,
'Cause the Good Lord was the architect.

Exodus 32:3-4

[3]So all the people took off the rings of gold which were in their ears, and brought them to Aaron. [4]And he received the gold at their hand, and fashioned it with a graving tool, and made a molten calf; and they said, "These are your gods, O Israel, who brought you up out of the land of Egypt!" (1)

The Golden Calf

The minute Moses' back was turned,
The candle at both ends was burned.
His people started out carousing,
Drinking, dancing, bawdy-housing.

This chapter in the Book discloses
Just how the entire scene shocked Moses,
But Moses' ire was most impassioned
At the golden calf that Aaron fashioned.

He shook his fist and started raving:
"You'll suffer for your misbehaving.
That precious metal was too vital
To waste it on a golden idol.

"That store of gold is now depleted,
Gold which dentists sorely needed
For each and every dental cavity,
So yours are sins of utmost gravity.

"And for those sins and misadventures,
You're gonna end up wearing dentures."

Now, why should I prevaricate?
The Good Book's got that story straight.

Leviticus 11:1-2, 12-13, 17, 19

[1]And the Lord said to Moses and Aaron, [2]"Say to the people of Israel, These are the living things which you may eat among all the beasts that are on the earth." (1)

[12]Whatsoever hath no fins nor scales in the waters, that is a detestable thing unto you.
[13]And these things ye shall have in detestation among the fowls; . . .

[17] . . . and the cormorant, and the great owl; . . .

[19]and the stork, . . . and the hoopoe, and the bat. (2)

Kosher Foods, à la Carte

Leviticus, we find, includes
A catalogue of kosher foods,
Including fish and fowl and meat
That the Lord allowed were fit to eat;
And others he declared taboo
To even the most hungry Jew.

Of fowl, the Good Lord made a lot;
Some are kosher, some are not.
The eagle, ossifrage* and bat
Cannot be eaten, and that's that!
What's more, one may not take a chance
On pelicans or cormorants,

And irrespective of their cravin',
They dassn't eat ibis or raven.
The stork, which serves a useful function,
Must be passed up without compunction.
The great owl, the Good Book's disclosin',
Cannot be eaten fresh or frozen.

Forbidden was the caterpillar,
Even as a 'tween-meals filler,
But, strangely, it was deemed quite proper
To nosh on cricket or grasshopper
(South of the border, it's been noted,
They're finger-lickin' chocolate-coated!).

Should a hostess find it necessary
To serve up breast of dromedary,
A Jewish guest must leave the scene
'Cause dromedaries are unclean,
And the same is true for cuts of swine,
Sauteed, braised or cooked in wine.**

→

If on pickled eel you're dotin',
Forget it — eels, too, are verboten.
But scales and fins are incontestable,
Though not, in every case, digestible,
For the piano scales have long been hated
No matter how well marinated.

Permitted is most any fish
The most observant Jew could wish,
But the Good Lord's dietary laws
Have omitted shrimp and lobster claws.
King crab legs are likewise offensive,
But that's quite all right — they're too expensive!

If all those "don't"s seem too confusing,
Remember just Who did the choosing!

---

*"Ossifrage," should you inquire,
Is another name for lammergeier.

**Exceptions creep in, *entre nous*,
When it comes to Southern barbecue.

Leviticus 13:2-3

[2]"When a man has on the skin of his body a swelling or an eruption or a spot, and it turns into a leprous disease on the skin . . . [3]and the priest shall examine the diseased spot on the skin of his body; and if the hair in the diseased spot has turned white and the disease appears to be deeper than the skin of his body, it is a leprous disease; when the priest has examined him he shall pronounce him unclean." (1)

No Dermatologists?

When the Good Book speaks of skin disease,
It brooks no ambiguities.
For every blemish, scab or spot,
It says what's leprous and what's not.
The high priests judged, so say these pages,
Which were benign and which contagious.

E.g., if sores were disappearing,
The priest refrained from interfering,
But if the lesions kept on growing,
The priest was seen to be all-knowing.
He'd hurry forth to intervene:
"It's leprosy! Unclean! Unclean!"

Of course, the priest was no physician,
But his was a secure position.
If he deemed leprous and nefarious
A blemish only urticarious*
And was called to task, the simple fact is
No one sued him for malpractice.

To say that priests were not too medical
Would seem to verge on the heretical,
And priests, then, needed no apologists
Just because there were no dermatologists.

So it doesn't pay to be too cynical
When the Good Book deals with matters clinical.

*Urticaria: hives.

Numbers 5:11-13, 22

[11]And the Lord said to Moses, [12]"Say to the people of Israel, If any man's wife goes astray and acts unfaithfully against him, [13]if a man lies with her carnally, and it is hidden from the eyes of her husband, and she is undetected though she has defiled herself, and there is no witness against her, . . ." (1)

[22]". . . a curse shall go into thy bowels, and make thy belly to swell, and thy thigh to fall away; and the woman shall say: 'Amen, amen.'" (3)

Out on a Limb with Hanky-Panky

The Good Book says the Lord gets cranky
About a little hanky-panky,
And this chapter, here, has underlined
Some details of His frame of mind:

If the husband were insanely jealous,
It made no difference, so they tell us,
If the wife were pure or desecrated;
She's guilty 'til exonerated.

Although her misdeeds were deniable,
The husband felt it justifiable
That he should cure each malefaction
With purges, which begat fast action.

The wife would get some obscure fever,
And by the time that it would leave her,
Although she had not done corruptly,
Her thigh would fall away abruptly.

"Not guilty" was the plea she'd planned on,
But she wouldn't have a leg to stand on,
And to be in this way reprimanded
Would seem to be a bit high-handed.*

But that husband who, through insecurity,
Cast doubts upon his own wife's purity
Would go unpunished for his error . . .
Those rules could not have been unfairer.

Today, such tales could lead to fights
By advocates of equal rights,
But only those who are misguided
Would call the Good Book's tale "one-sided."

---

*The mixed metaphor — about extremities —
Is a vice for which there are few remedies.

Numbers 11:18-20, 31, 33

18"'. . . Therefore the Lord will give you meat, and you shall eat. 19You shall not eat one day, or two days, or five days, or ten days, or twenty days, 20but a whole month, until it comes out at your nostrils and becomes loathsome to you, . . .'"

31 . . . brought quails from the sea . . . about two cubits deep on the face of the earth.

33 . . . and the Lord smote the people with a very great plague. (1)

The All-Quail Diet

If the Good Book has that story right —
Manna morning, noon and night —
I know just why they chose to riot
For wholesale changes in their diet.

They clamored for repasts complete
With ample servings of fresh meat.
But Moses' minions needed humbling,
For the Lord had had enough of grumbling,

And the Lord gained some small satisfaction
By making quails the chief attraction.
Quails for breakfast and for luncheon,
And the frig held only quails for munchin'.

Quails were stacked two cubits thick —
They were, one could say, plethoric.
They fed on quail stew every night,
Until they all quailed at the sight.

The Good Lord, having called their bluff,
Decided that they had had enough,
And He sent a plague down on those acres,
To punish all the troublemakers.

Although such stories sound horrendous,
They're not intended to offend us,
'Cause the Good Book just presents the facts
And remains immune to all attacks.

Numbers 20:8

[8]"Take the rod, and assemble the congregation, you and Aaron your brother, and tell the rock before their eyes to yield its water; so you shall bring water out of the rock for them; . . ." (1)

Water from a Rock

The Chosen People had been pondering
The years that they had spent in wandering,
And they started giving Moses static.
Their life, they said, was too nomadic,
And they grumbled, "Where's this Land of Plenty?
Could it be that there isn't any?

"We'd welcome help from any quarter,
But what we need right now is water."
Now Moses heard his band complaining;
The trip was hard and it wasn't raining,
And his brother, Aaron, thought they oughtter
Ask the Lord to bring them water.

The Lord's reply was quite surprisin':
"See that rock on the horizon?
If you'll address it with gentility,
That boulder will have the ability
To gush forth in a stream torrential —
At least, it once had that potential."

But patience had been wearing thin
For Moses and his next of kin.
He stepped up to that stone outcropping,
Raised his staff, and without stopping,
He gave that rock an awful clout,
And H_20 came pouring out!

The Lord said, "Moses, I'll be candid.
What you did was too heavy-handed.
You must have thought that I was kidding,
But since you did not heed My bidding,
These words, then, are what I command:
'You shall never reach the Promised Land.'"

Consensus would be, at this time,
The punishment didn't fit the crime,
But the Good Book says his fate was sealed,
And the case was, therefore, not appealed.

Deuteronomy 21:18-19, 22:5

[18]If a man have a stubborn and rebellious son, that will not hearken to the voice of his father, or the voice of his mother, and though they chasten him, will not hearken unto them; [19]then shall his father and his mother lay hold on him, . . .

[5]A woman shall not wear that which pertaineth unto a man, neither shall a man put on a woman's garment; . . . (2)

So Many Laws for a Minority?

The Good Book's Book of Deuteronomy
Reveals God's plans for the autonomy
Of the Hebrew people He'd protected
With many more rules than expected.
(In case some of you may have wondered,
There were in excess of six hundred.)

"Once you cross the River Jordan,"
The Lord said, "I shall be recordin'
All those whose sins are overriding
My orders to be law-abiding."

There were rules for errant sons and daughters,
And rules forbade polluting waters,
Rules enjoining narcissism
And against all forms of criticism,
Rules for pseudointellectuals
And also bans on homosexuals,

Rules about your brother's ox
And, very likely, chicken pox.
Rules to fit a common criminal
And bans on obscene thoughts subliminal,
Bans on men in women's clothes —
Vice versa, too, as you'd suppose.

Those laws were meant for all to keep
From day one to "that dreamless sleep,"
And the Hebrews more than once lamented
That no rule could be circumvented.

We don't doubt the Good Book's authority,
But . . . so many laws for a minority?

Deuteronomy 22:23-25, 27

[23]"If there is a betrothed virgin, and a man meets her in the city and lies with her, [24]then you shall bring them both out to the gate of that city, and you shall stone them to death with stones, . . . [25]But if in the open country a man meets a young woman who is betrothed . . . then only the man who lay with her shall die.

[27] . . . though the betrothed young woman cried for help there was no one to rescue her." (1)

Rules for Vacillating Virgins

In Deuteronomy, there's explanation
Of the rules for any situation.
There were just deserts for light adultery
And punishments for sirens sultry,

But the rules that you'll find most astonishing
Are those directed at admonishing
Maidens who showed vacillation
In a compromising situation.

If one were ravished in a city,
The Lord said He would show no pity
'Cause had she wished for intervention,
She could have screamed to get attention;

But if the knowledge she were getting
Occurred in a suburban setting,
They'd execute the rogue who did it,
But she'd most likely be acquitted,

For though she had yelled bloody murder,
The theory is: who would have heard her?
From these laws, maidens soon were learning,
In dalliances, to be discerning.

When yielding to the urge to frolic,
Be sure the setting is bucolic.
Better yet, while still prenuptial,
Conceal those assets most voluptual.

And it's doubtful you'd have the audacity
To question the Good Book's veracity.

Deuteronomy 25:11

[11]"When men fight with one another, and the wife of the one draws near to rescue her husband from the hand of him who is beating him, and puts out her hand and seizes him by the private parts, then shall you cut off her hand; your eye shall have no pity." (1)

No Holds Barred

The Lord gave Moses regulations
About all sorts of confrontations,
And when two neighbors fall to fighting —
Whatever quarrel they are deciding —
There are a few rules we should mention
About illegal intervention.

If one combatant's wife jumps in
To play the role of heroine,
Injects herself into the wrangling
And grabs and twists whatever's dangling,
'Twould violate the Good Lord's wishes,
For He frowns on deeds so injudicious.

Although the wives from both the houses
Could place side bets upon their spouses,
Bans were placed on interfering
By grabbing items so endearing.
Since Moses said the Lord forbid it,
Off must come the hand that did it.

Now, such a three-way confrontation
Boggles the imagination:

If she just dives in and starts groping,
Things might not turn out as she's hoping.
With both combatants intertwined,
It could be difficult to find
Just what's concealed beneath the skirting
Without one of the two men hurting.

If the wife just plunges in and grasps
And one man lets out a scream and gasps
And his mind goes blank and his ears are ringing
And he can almost hear the angels singing
And his toes are curled and fists clenched tight
And his hair is standing straight upright
*

And his screams are laden with profanity
And his actions border on insanity
And his eyes protrude, his face turns bluish,
And he can't remember if he's Jewish
And he sputters just like a volcano
And, abruptly, he's a boy soprano
And he twists and turns in mortal terror . . .
It's just possible she made an error!

Amid confusion, as they battled,
If she's the one becoming rattled
And when, at last, she is desisting
('Cause she'd been doing all the twisting)
And, rising, looks down at the fallen,
What greets her eyes could be appallin',

For the scream could well have emanated
From the man to whom she was related,
And she'd see, 'mongst tunics and torn blouses,
Those mangled parts were her own spouse's!

Yet even though her wrath descended
On the wrong man, she'd be apprehended,
And though the battle were a stand-off,
The judge would order, "Chop her hand off!"

But possibly the judge would spare her
If she agreed she'd made an error
And simply reached in with abandon
For those things she could get her hand on.
He'd deem her punishment sufficient:
Her spouse no longer heir-conditioned.

~ Moral ~

Although the Good Book seems quite wordy
In warning women who fight dirty,
This story leaves us with a moral:
If you should get into a quarrel
And your wife's convinced you could be better
And tries to help, don't let her!

Deuteronomy 34:1, 4

[1]And Moses went up from the plains of Moab to Mount Nebo, to the top of Pisgah, which is opposite Jericho. And the Lord showed him all the land, Gilead as far as Dan, . . .

[4]And the Lord said to him, ". . . I have let you see it with your eyes, but you shall not go over there." (1)

Moses Sees the Promised Land

In the Good Book, you may recollect
That Moses knew what to expect
When the years of wandering were ended
'Cause the Good Lord, having been offended,
Had promised that His chief lawgiver
Would never cross the Jordan River.

It often puzzles men of learning
Why, after all of his sojourning,
He was allowed, the book recites,
To see that Land from Pisgah's heights
But really never had much hope
Of getting closer than that slope.*

Thereby lies the controversy:
The Good Lord is a Lord of mercy
And since He's known to be forgiving,
Why not let Moses, while still living,
Cash in on his years of toil
And set foot on that Promised Soil?

But he never reached the land of plenty,
And he passed on at one-hundred twenty.

The Good Lord's workings are mysterious,
So what Moses said must have been serious.

---

*Although not phrased in the vernacular,
The Talmud's version's more spectacular,
For it would have us understand
That Moses saw the Promised Land.
The Lord gave Moses one small peek
Into a sight that was unique:
He saw God's Chosen People climb
Through adversity, to the end of time.

The Prophets

Joshua 6:5

[5]And when they make a long blast with the ram's horn, as soon as you hear the sound of the trumpet, then all the people shall shout with a great shout; and the wall of the city will fall down flat, . . . (1)

The Walls of Jericho

The Good Book says, as you all know,
That Joshua marched 'round Jericho.
Seven times around that wall he passed;
Then he gave his horn a mighty blast,
And Jericho's walls came tumbling down,
So the Good book says, right on that town.

"They didn't make them like they used to,"
So rubble's what it was reduced to.
Perhaps the builder was too frugal
If that wall was brought down by a bugle.

But the Good Book's got that story pat,
So it must have happened just like that.

Joshua 10:6-7

[6]And the men of Gibeon sent unto Joshua to the camp to Gilgal, saying: '. . . save us and help us; for all the kings of the Amorites that dwell in the hill-country are gathered together against us.' [7]So Joshua went up from Gilgal, he, and all the people of war with him, and all the mighty men of valour. (2)

Joshua Smites the Amorites

In the book of Joshua, scholars wrote
How Joshua, with his great sword, smote
Those monarchs who had the audacity
To question his downright pugnacity.

But the Amorites formed an alliance
To use their military science
And do unto the Jews their worst
Before the Jews got to them first.

They girt their loins, strapped on their swords
And reached the Jordan in great hordes,
The officers in golden chariots;
Behind them marched the proletariat.

The Amoritic plan of battle:
Slaughter all the Jews like cattle.
They planned to use techniques amphibian
And thus besiege the town of Gibeon.

They shouted taunts and hurled insults
And showered stones from catapults.
At first, the Hebrews met that violence
With what you might call stony silence.

Though it appeared the kings were winning,
The Hebrews had not had their inning,
For the Good Lord, working at a distance,
Provided Joshua with assistance.

It's obvious who won those fights,
For today there are no Amorites!

Joshua 10:12-13

[12] . . . 'Sun, stand thou still upon Gibeon;
And thou, Moon, in the valley of Aijalon.'
[13]And the sun stood still, and the moon stayed,
Until the nation had avenged themselves of their enemies. (2)

Joshua Makes the Sun Stand Still

In the Good Book, no detail's omitted
In telling just how Joshua did it.
The Lord said, "Though the job's laborious,
Just hang on, Josh, you'll be victorious."

The battle's fury waxed and waned,
But the outcome had been foreordained,
For the battle had to be concluded
Before the Sabbath eve intruded.

On that day, it would be profanity
To slaughter thousands of humanity,
A day when one should love thy neighbor
And shun all forms of manual labor.

His battle tactics were empirical;
He simply called upon a miracle.
He said, "Oh, Lord, don't frown on us,
And let the sun beam down on us

"Until our mop-up detail smites
The last remaining Amorites!"
The sun, the Good Book says, obeyed,
And the Sabbath nightfall thus was stayed.

Since to fight on Sabbath was a crime,
Josh invented daylight saving time!

Now, the Good Book's accurate to the minute,
So you'd best believe what's written in it.

Judges 16:4-5

[4]And it came to pass afterward, that he loved a woman in the valley of Sorek, whose name was Delilah. [5]And the lords of the Philistines came up unto her, and said unto her: 'Entice him, and see wherein his great strength lieth, . . .' (2)

Samson Brings Down the House

Samson's hair was long and curly,
And Delilah was his favorite girlie,
But her loyalties were Philistinian,
Which is logical, in my opinion,
Since she plotted Samson's liquidation
For a handsome cash consideration.

She knew the value of a dollar,
And, sadly, he was no Rhodes scholar.
As his curly head lay in her lap,
Delilah cooly sprung her trap.
That very night, his locks were shorn
Precisely as his foes had sworn.

The Phillies cried, "We've got him, sure!"
But they were slightly premature.
Those plotters diabolical
Forgot that each hair follicle
Would undergo regeneration
And give rise to retaliation.

So the Good Book tells us in this thriller
How our hero firmly grasped each pillar
Of the house where jeering throngs collected
And, with his strength now resurrected,
Did what no one there expected:
With just one shove, completely wrecked it!

Each word is true that I'm reciting,
'Cause the Good Book's got it there in writing.

I Samuel 17:37, 50, 18:12, 14-15

[37] . . . And Saul said to David, "Go, and the Lord be with you!"

[50]So David prevailed over the Philistine with a sling and with a stone, and struck the Philistine, and killed him; . . .

[12]Saul was afraid of David, because the Lord was with him but had departed from Saul.

[14]And David had success in all his undertakings; for the Lord was with him. [15]And when Saul saw that he had great success, he stood in awe of him. (1)

David Has His Fling

The Good Book at this point relates
How King Saul sought for surrogates
In case he should encounter losses
Against the Philistine's colossus.

Said Saul, "I'd rather have the pleasure
Of taking big Goliath's measure,
And it's obvious I'm more than willin'
To clash with the aforesaid villain.

"Though at my hands he'd be a goner,
I fear I must forego that honor.
Though my urge for battle is acute,
I'll just have to find a substitute."

To show young David his affection,
He sent him in big "G's" direction.
Goliath, taken by surprise,
Got it right between the eyes.

Cried Dave, "King Saul, in your dominion
You now have one less Philistinian."
And King Saul suffered by comparison
In front of his whole army garrison.

His face got red, and he grew furious;
He promised Dave a fate injurious,
Which would reduce his popularity . . .
Saul wasn't famous for his charity!

And the Good Book's pages clearly tell us
What happens when a king gets jealous,
For King Saul tried to do his worst.
It's all spelled out in Samuel First.

I Samuel 18:25

[25]And Saul said: 'Thus shall ye say to David: The king desireth not any dowry, but a hundred foreskins of the Philistines, to be avenged of the king's enemies.' For Saul thought to make David fall by the hand of the Philistines. (2)

Two Hundred Foreskins!

Now, King Saul was no "rose geranium,"
And when he got it in his cranium
That there was a pronounced disparity
In his and David's popularity,
He sent Dave, in a ploy transparent,
Upon a suicidal errand.

Said Saul, "If you would please my Royalty,
Just bring me back, to show your loyalty,
One hundred foreskins, on condition:
They all come from the opposition.
Just bring me back one hundred of 'em
To show the Phillies we don't love 'em."

When Saul sent David on that mission,
It was no scouting expedition.
Said Dave, "No problem, lord and master;
I'll create my own one-man disaster,
And I'll also add, with greatest pleasure,
Another hundred for good measure."

Still, two unanswered questions linger
About Saul and his ballad singer.
To start with, I have some misgivings
About the foreskins — dead or living?
And just how would they be procured
If all the Philistines demurred?

For those were times when circumcision
Was not performed with great precision;
In those days, there was quite a chasm
'Twixt skill and sheer enthusiasm.
But there still linger further questions
About which I have some suggestions.

King Saul, it seems, was now confronted
With more foreskins than he had wanted.
We're certain, without reservation,
They weren't used for transplantation;
The Jews would not, in my opinion,
Use foreskins that were Philistinian.

Was there a plan with which Saul flirted
To have each Philistine converted?
A mass conversion he'd be pleased at,
And two hundred's nothing to be sneezed at.
Although their tongue was Aramaic,
Their other end would be Hebraic.

Now, this tale should cause us no distress,
'Cause it's in the Good Book — more or less.

I Samuel 19:9-10

[9]Then an evil spirit from the Lord came upon Saul, as he sat in his house with his spear in his hand; and David was playing the lyre. [10]And Saul sought to pin David to the wall with the spear; but he eluded Saul, so that he struck the spear into the wall. And David fled, and escaped. (1)

Saul Tries to Skewer David

Temper, temper, Monarch Saul.
It wasn't nice of you at all
To try to pin Dave to the wall.

Thank God you're only fair to middling
With that spear on which you're wittling,
The result of which was that you missed him.
Didja get it, Saul, out of your system?

Temper, temper, rant and rave —
You're king, and kings don't misbehave.
Deeds like yours show your depravity;
We view them with the utmost gravity.

Forget those evil plans you're brewing.
That spear could have been your undoing
Because you know how folks would view it
Had you not missed him when you threw it.

Temper, temper — need I mention —
You should watch your hypertension.
If you'd forego that lethal weapon,
Things like that just could not happen.

You'd simply go on with your loathing,
Bite your nails and rend your clothing,
And even though you'd still be furious,
It's certain to be less injurious.

Temper, temper, fast unravelin'.
You need more practice with that javelin.
If you missed Dave from that short distance,
How did you slay all those Philistince?

But as the Good Book has made mention,
The Lord negated your intention
And demonstrated how He thwarts
An evil monarch's game of darts.

I Samuel 24:3-4

[3] . . . there was a cave; and Saul went in to relieve himself. Now David and his men were sitting in the innermost parts of the cave. [4] . . . Then David arose and stealthily cut off the skirt of Saul's robe. (1)

Squatters' Rights

The Good Book, in Samuel, leaves the impression
That David's demise was Saul's greatest obsession.
Since Dave's troops were few and were not battle-ready,
They hid in a cave in a place called Engedi.

Hot on their heels came King Saul and his legions,
Not too familiar with Engedi's regions.
No privies were visible on the horizon,
So when nature called, Saul began improvisin'.

He found a cave nearby and hurried inside it
(You could say, in retrospect, Saul was misguided) —
The very same cave in which David was hidden!
He could have killed Saul, but as we know, he didn't.

As King Saul was squatting in deep concentration,
Dave snipped off his skirt, much to Saul's consternation.
Saul looked up at David. Said David, "So there!
Your villainous plotting has now been laid bare.

"Here, take back your tunic — allow me to pin it —
And forget your vendetta, because you can't win it."
So regicide was in that manner averted;
The issue, you might say, has thusly been skirted.

Just how is it, David, that you were so crafty
That you left Saul squatting there, undraped and drafty?
But we know that Saul's garment had been amputated;
It's there in First Samuel, unexpurgated.

~ Moral ~

There's a moral to glean from this story of Saul:
Don't opt for a cave when you hear nature's call
Or you'll be ensnared in some pitiful plights
If the cave boasts a tenant who has squatter's rights.

I Samuel 28:3, 5, 7

[3]Now Samuel had died, . . . And Saul had put the mediums and the wizards out of the land.

[5]When Saul saw the army of the Philistines, he was afraid, . . .

[7]Then Saul said to his servants, "Seek out for me a woman who is a medium, that I may go to her and inquire of her." And his servants said to him, "Behold, there is a medium at Endor." (1)

The Witch of Endor

The Good Book says, here, that King Saul's reign was ended,
But not in the way that the King had intended.
The Philistine armies for vengeance were yearning
And felt that, at long last, their luck might be turning,
So they strapped on their swords and began their invasion
With thousands of Phillies, to suit the occasion.

King Saul cried, "This looks like the moment of truth!"
So he sought a soothsayer to say him a sooth.
Now, Saul, you remember, had banished soothsayers,
Relying instead on his faith and his prayers,
But this time he panicked and called for a seeress.
He screamed to his aides, "Go find one who lives near us."

Disguised, they rode off to the valley of Endor
And sought out a witch of the feminine gender.
"I hear," said King Saul, "as a witch, you're omniscient,
So one incantation should be quite sufficient.
Just resurrect Samuel, wherever he's hidden,"
And the great witch of Endor did just that — no kiddin'!

Sam rose from his grave, as the king had been wishin',
And Saul put two questions to Sam's apparition:
"Will history, as in the past, be repeated?
Will I be the victor or finally defeated?"

And a voice came to Saul from beyond death's broad chasm:
"I have good news and bad news," said Sam's ectoplasm.
"The good news," it said, "in the message I'm sending
Is you needn't worry about the war's ending.
The bad news: your people will be deep in sorrow
'Cause you will be joining me sometime tomorrow."

And Samuel's forecast came true, it is written,
For Saul, on the very next morning, was smitten.

~ Moral ~

The lesson we learn from King Saul's sad demise is
Do not waste your time on soothsayers' advices.
If you are aware that you're greatly outnumbered,
Get rid of all baggage with which you're encumbered,
And that includes witches, whom you should be shunning.
Just head for the hills while you can, and keep running.

II Samuel 6:14-15, 23

[14]And David danced before the Lord with all his might; and David was girded with a linen ephod. [15]So David and all of the house of Israel brought up the ark of the Lord with shouting, and with the sound of the horn.

[23]And Michal the daughter of Saul had no child to the day of her death. (1)

King David's Flying Ephod

When David ruled Zion, he chose a committee
To transport the ark of the Lord to the city.
The ark was brought into the city's enclosure,
And, drunk with emotion, he lost his composure.

Clad in an ephod of finely spun linen,
A loose fitting apron with no underpinnin',
As David danced wildly, the ephod went flying,
With results that were startling, there is no denying.

In a mad burst of frenzy, King David was swirling
While the ephod, fit loosely, continued unfurling,
So that each of his subjects could view at their leisure
An unusual glimpse of the monarchal treasure.

From her window, disconsolate, Michal was watching
As her husband, King David, engaged in debauching.
Imagine the poor lady's humiliation
As her handmaidens looked on in sheer fascination.

With the revelry ended, King David, exhausted,
Returned to the palace, where he was accosted
By Michal, face puffy and eyes red from weeping:
"The living room sofa is where you'll be sleeping."

And the Good Book informs us that, at her insistence,
From that same night forward, Michal kept her distance.

Could Saul have, in some way, reached out from the grave
To embarrass the king and make him misbehave?
Although such a notion may strike you as eerie,
It is just dialectic — no more than a theory.

Why not? Even stranger adventures are liable
To turn up if you will just study the Biable.

II Samuel 14:25-26, 18:9, 14

[25]Now in all Israel there was no one so much to be praised for his beauty as Absalom; . . . [26]And when he cut the hair of his head (for at the end of every year he used to cut it; . . .), he weighed the hair of his head, two hundred shekels by the king's weight.

[9]And Absalom chanced to meet the servants of David. Absalom was riding upon his mule, and the mule went under the thick branches of a great oak, and his head caught fast in the oak, and he was left hanging between heaven and earth, while the mule that was under him went on.

[14]And he [Joab] *took three darts in his hand, and thrust them into the heart of Absalom, while he was still alive in the oak.* (1)

Absalom's Hair-Raising Demise

The Good Book informs us, in Samuel second,
That the finger of fate to young Absalom beckoned,

But that finger might not have been aimed at his coffin
If he'd made a trip to the barber more often,

For Absalom had his locks trimmed but once yearly,
Eccentric behavior for which he paid dearly.

He passed under trees which he didn't see clearly
And was caught in a terebinth by his hair, merely.

Without a hair clipper, he hung there suspended
And was skewered like shish kabob ere the day ended.

Oh, Absalom, Absalom, it's past all believing
The web of destruction your tresses were weaving.

And the horrible fate which cut off your existence
You could have been spared, with a crew cut, for instance.

~ Moral ~

The lesson is clear: to insure your longevity,
Your hair, much like wit, should be known for its brevity.

II Samuel 14:26, Judges 16:17

[26]*And when he* [Absalom] *cut the hair of his head (for at the end of every year he used to cut it; . . .)* (1)

[17]*'. . . if I be shaven, then my strength will go from me, and I shall become weak, and be like any other man.'* (2)

The Long and the Short of It

The Good Book sends signals that could be confusing;
They seem to depend on which verse you're perusing.
It's true that if Absalom's hair were less flowing,
He could have seen, one would think, where he was going.

It was Absalom's fate — perhaps allegorical —
That he was too casual in matters tonsorial.

But what about Samson, whose strength we still herald?
When he had his hair cut, his life was imperiled.
His hair, had it stayed in an uncut condition,
Would surely have brushed aside all opposition.

Though these hair-raising tales are both sober and tense,
The Good Book sits perched on both sides of the fence.

~ Moral ~

So the lesson we learn from this pithy polemic:
If you're bald, the question becomes academic.

I Kings 3:24-25

[24]And the king said, "Bring me a sword." So a sword was brought before the king. [25]And the king said, "Divide the living child in two, and give half to the one, and half to the other." (1)

A Split Decision

The Book of Kings is packed with action,
And Solomon is the chief attraction.
No king, in those days, in reality
Could match King Solomon's mentality.
One simple story probes the vortex
Of his oversized cerebral cortex.

Two women, each a female parent,
Laid claim to the same heir apparent.

Sol's judgment was quite unexpected:
He ruled the tot should be bisected,
While the mothers looked on, horror-stricken,
To see which mother first "turned chicken."

And the one who pleaded, Sol decided,
To keep the baby undivided
Would win out in the courtroom drama
'Cause she would be the rightful mama.

Now, Solomon's ploy to choose the mother
Resolved one question, raised another:
If neither mother had objected,
Would the king have done the unexpected?

Would the sword have come down with finality,
Creating a split personality?
Would the *coup de grâce* have been administered,
With one half dextered, the other sinistered?

About that, I don't mind confessing,
The Good Book simply leaves us guessing.

I Kings 11:3

[3]He had seven hundred wives, princesses, and three hundred concubines; and his wives turned away his heart. (1)

Condominia in Abyssinia?

Throughout most of his royal regime,
King Solomon stood in high esteem
Because, as the Good Book advises,
Of all the kings, he was the wisest.

His wealth, we're told, by far exceeded
The wealth of any who'd preceded
(He had more shekels in his vault than
John Paul Getty or the late Sam Walton).

He owned a glut of condominia
From Jerusalem to Abyssinia,
In Roman styles and also Grecian,
In varying stages of completion.

He had gold coins and tons of jewels,
And, of course, he had two swimming pools,
Along with very large amounts
Of money in Swiss bank accounts.

The good king's wealth had other facets,
Surpassing all his liquid assets:
Seven hundred wives had he and treasured,
And that is how true wealth was measured.

He had the largest of all houses,
Packed to the rafters with his spouses.
Its rooms for functions amatorious
Were grander than Waldorf-Astoria's.

The Good Book says he had designs
On some three hundred concubines.
No man could do aught but admire
The magnitude of his desire.

We know that Solomon really had 'em
Because the Good Book has that datum.

II Kings 2:8, 13-14

[8]Then Elijah took his mantle, and rolled it up, and struck the water, and the water was parted to the one side and to the other, till the two of them could go over on dry ground.

[13]And he [Elisha] *took up the mantle of Elijah that had fallen from him, and went back and stood on the bank of the Jordan. [14] . . . and struck the water, saying "Where is the Lord, the God of Elijah?" And when he had struck the water, the water was parted to the one side and to the other; and Elisha went over.* (1)

Elijah Fordin' the Jordan

R.I.P. 1994

That was something Moses started
When the Red Sea waters parted.
It was just a piece of cake for God's lawgiver.
Said Elijah, "Nothing to it!
Moses did it — I can do it!
And that's how I'll get across the Jordan River."

That same morning, when he woke up,
Elijah rolled his cloak up
With intent to walk across the river bed.
Lo and behold! Repeat performance!
Strolled across with bone-dry garments,
With his disciples close behind, so it is said.

Then spake Elisha, his disciple
(It is right there in the Bible),
"I'm across the Jordan, and I must get back.
I'll use the mantle of my mentor,
Smite the water, and then enter.
I watched him, and I think I've got the knack."

And having thusly spoken,
He picked up Elijah's cloak, and
He smote the Jordan using his technique.
Once again the river parted.
Elisha took one look and started,
Hotfooting it across there, so to speak.

* * *

→

Now, it happened just last week
At a nearby swollen creek,
Would-be prophets tried to duplicate that deed,
Which wasn't very prudent,
Even for a bible student . . .
From these headstones, clearly, they did not succeed.

Ezekiel 37:1-4

[1]The hand of the Lord was upon me, and the Lord c...
spirit, and set me down in the midst of the valley, and it ...
bones; [2]and He caused me to pass by them round about, and, be...
there were very many in the open valley, and, lo, they were very dry.
[3]And He said unto me: 'Son of man, can these bones live?' . . .
[4]Then he said unto me: 'Prophesy over these bones, and say unto them: O ye dry bones, hear the word of the Lord: . . .' (2)

The Valley of Dry Bones

In Ezekiel, the Book intones
About the valley of dry bones.

The Lord spoke, and Ezekiel trembled
Because those bones lay disassembled,
Awaiting their reincarnation
From their state of desiccation.

The Lord said, "Zeke, I'll be relying
On you to do some prophesying
'Cause you will have the job of proving
That you can get those dry bones moving."
Said Zeke, "When You speak, I obey,"
And he prophesied without delay.

He jumped up and began declaiming,
And his message he was aiming
At the host of little parcels
Of assorted metatarsals.

As Ezekial was sermonizing,
All those bones began arising,
Moving off in all directions
To find appropriate connections.

Each skeleton was reconstructed
At the meetings Zeke conducted,
Their status quo ante thus restored
Through the intervention of the Lord.

So this "bare bones" tale gives evidence
About the Lord's Omnipotence,
For it happened with rapidity
In that valley of aridity.

Micah 4:3-4

[3] . . . And they shall beat their swords into plowshares,
And their spears into pruning-hooks;
Nation shall not lift up sword against nation,
Neither shall they learn war any more.
[4]But they shall sit every man under his vine and under his fig-tree;
And none shall make them afraid; . . . (2)

One Fig Tree Per Capita

The Lord said, "Armageddon tired
Of all this constant fighting,
So, Micah, prophesy for peace,
And make it sound inviting."

So Micah promptly prophesied:
"And it shall come to pass . . .
A world of peace, et cetera . . ."
But where is it, alas?

For the nations say to Micah, "Sir,
We buy what you are peddling,
But, first, we have a few old scores
That still require some settling."

Though Micah's words would guarantee
One whole fig tree per capita,
The fig trees will outnumber us
If peace does not come rapider.

Such caveats move us to say
If it happens, then so be it,
But the odds are that not one of us
Will be around to see it.

Joel 4:10

[10]Beat your plowshares into swords,
And your pruning-hooks into spears; . . . (2)

A Prophecy "*Umgekehrt*"

As this chapter will assert,
Things are sometimes "*umgekehrt*"
(In German, that means, roughly, "turned around").
Joel's words, you will take note,
Call to mind another quote,
Those phrases for which Micah was renowned.

'Cause Joel's words preceded Micah's,
One odd notion seems to strike us:
Just how could he have stolen Micah's thunder?
Since he was intent on wars,
Did he mix his metaphors?
How did he pull it off? It makes you wonder.

What poor farmer could afford
A plowshare made into a sword
And a spear made from a pruning hook? No thanks!
If that is what they planned on,
All the farmers would abandon
All their lands and turn their tractors into tanks.

God could not have wanted war —
We are certain on that score.
Was Joel done in by the printing press?
Still, if that chapter could be read
While you're standing on your head,
It possibly would make sense — more or less.

Amos 4:9, 8:9-10

[9]I have smitten you with blasting and mildew;
The multitude of your gardens and your vineyards
And your fig-trees . . .
Hath the palmer-worm devoured; . . .

[9]And it shall come to pass in that day,
Saith the Lord God,
That I will cause the sun to go down at noon, . . .
[10] . . . And I will bring up sackcloth upon all loins,
And baldness upon every head; . . . (2)

No Bed of Roses

Among the prophets, Amos
May not be very famous,
But he's not a prophet given to banality.
A man in his position
Is bound to have a mission:
God's messenger in battling immorality.

In Amos' vision, he defined
Just what the Good Lord had in mind:
There were earthquakes, floods and locusts, at His pleasure,
Also famine, stench and fire,
Said the Good Lord's prophesier,
And threw in a total eclipse for good measure.

Added Amos, "I forgot —
All the mountaintops will rot,
And the crops will die because of worms and mildew,
And the Good Lord will include
Involuntary servitude —
That's exactly what I have been told He will do."

But even more outrageous,
As you'll find out in these pages,
A dandruff plague will smite all those transgressors —
One great sea of shiny crania
From Eilat to Mesopotamia.
They'll look like Martians to all their successors.

But the House of Jacob will be saved,
Though it's true they misbehaved,
And their suffering was not what you'd call "hairy."
Still, for all their living days,
All the sinners wore toupees,
So if you sin, you'd do well to be wary.

Isaiah, Job or Amos —
Makes no difference what his name is —
Each prophet has some pearls of wisdom for you.
But Amos is so scary
That when you turn to prayer, he
Will guarantee his prophecies won't bore you.

Jonah 2:1

[1]And the Lord prepared a great fish to swallow up Jonah; and Jonah was in the belly of the fish three days and three nights. (2)

A Whale of a Tale

The Good Book sets forth, in detail,
How Jonah wound up in the whale.
But there are scholars who demur
'Cause certain facts remain obscure.

One explanation which persists
Comes straight from dental theorists.
They state that one of Jonah's ventures
Was studying mammalian dentures.
He checked into that whale's dentition
And didn't ask the whale's permission.

He just said, "Moby, open wide,"
And, presto, Jonah was inside,
Which goes to show what hazards lurk
When you're swallowed up in your own work.

Just take the Good Book's word, albeit
You may not have been there to see it.

Haggai 1:3-4

[3]Then came the word of the Lord by Haggai the prophet, saying: [4]'Is it a time for you yourselves to dwell in your ceiled houses, while this house lieth waste?' (2)

A Minor Doing the Driving?

It isn't clear why
There's a Book of Haggai,
But it's there in the Bible, so read it.
Said the Lord to Haggai,
"Won't you please prophesy
For My Temple, which I'd like completed?"

Now the Good Book reveals
That the Jews dragged their heels.
"We don't enjoy working in granite."
But Haggai said, "Rebuild it
'Cause the Good Lord hath willed it,"
So they donned their hard hats and began it.

Through the Lord's words, as given,
The Hebrews were driven,
Including Haggai, the diviner.
But Haggai, though surviving,
Was not the one driving
'Cause, remember, he was just a minor.

The Writings

Psalms 49:11

[11]For he seeth that wise men die,
The fool and the brutish together perish,
And leave their wealth to others. (2)

No Pockets in Shrouds

There are psalms accompanied by lyre
And some that need a mighty choir.

There's the forty-ninth, the point of which is
Don't boast too much about your riches,
For the rich and poor, it is inferred,
Have the same net worth when they're interred.

At the IRS, it should be noted,
The forty-ninth is never quoted
'Cause even though you're in the grave,
They'll take each nickel that you save.

If you'd outwit the IRS,
It might not be amiss, I guess,
To reappraise this entire topic
And be a bit more philanthropic.

As for the poor: those in that stratum
Need not read this psalm verbatim.

Psalms 78:2

[2]I will open my mouth with a parable;
I will utter dark sayings concerning days of old. (2)

Psalms of Joy When the Market Rises

In the Book of Psalms, you'll find solutions
To avoid all sorts of retributions.
There are psalms for winter and for summer,
Psalms when life has been a bummer,
Psalms when life has held surprises,
And psalms of joy when the market rises.

There's a maskil,* noted for its brevity,
And psalms of praise for your longevity.
There are miktams** that evoke looks quizzical
And a psalm for when you pass your physical.

There's a maskil for when houseguests leave
And a psalm for use on New Year's Eve.

So if you wish to be devout
And want your prayers to have some clout,
Just polish up on your comportment
By delving into this assortment.

No matter what your choice of creeds,
You'll find one tailored to your needs,
And all of them you'll find inviting
'Cause they're in the Book of Psalms in writing.

---

*In Psalms, there's something called a "maskil,"
An elusive sort of rascal
Not found in any dictionary,
And that seems extraordinary.

**And there's a "miktam," in addition,
About which I have a suspicion
That it relates to a large chorus . . .
But it's not in Roget's Thesaurus.

Psalms 109:2-3, 9-11, 13

[2] . . . They have spoken unto me with a lying tongue.
[3]They compassed me about also with words of hatred,
And fought against me without cause.

[9]Let his children be fatherless
And his wife a widow.
[10] Let his children be vagabonds, and beg;
And let them seek their bread out of their desolate places.
[11]Let the creditor distrain all that he hath;
And let strangers make spoil of his labour.

[13]Let his posterity be cut off;
In the generation following let their name be blotted out. (2)

Invectives Pour Forth in a Torrent

Despite the Good Book's pious phrases,
There are some questions which it raises,
And in this psalm, you'll find a few surprises.
Invectives you might find abhorrent
Appear to pour forth in a torrent
Without the slightest hint of compromises.

King David's foes were less than gracious;
Their blows were verbal and mendacious.
The King, of course, responded with asperity.
He called down direful imprecations
On all his foes and their relations,
Including nephews, aunts and their posterity.

The Bible student has two choices:
Could David have been hearing voices,
Or did he have good reason to be wary?
The King's detractors — were they vicious,
Or were his curses all capricious?
Did he imagine every adversary?

David was, when young, so gentle.
Were his afflictions wholly mental?
Were all his problems psychoanalytical?
It could well have been a neurosis,
But with no clear-cut diagnosis,
We'll take the Good Book's words and not be critical.

➔

Although invectives fill this psalm,
A lesson may be learned therefrom,
    The gist of which is: words need not upset you.
Still, there's one truth you can't avoid:
Although you may be paranoid,
    It doesn't mean that they're not out to get you.

Proverbs 4:16

*[16]For they sleep not, except they have done evil;
And their sleep is taken away, unless they
cause someone to fall.* (2)

The Thief Is Caught Napping

The Book of Proverbs seems ambivalent
By making crime and sleep equivalent,
For this verse appears to be disclosing
That the evil-doer does the dozing.

The Good Book's words are unassailable,
Yet certain theories are available.
You're dozing — dreams are just subliminal —
Then through the window climbs a criminal.

He burglarizes your abode;
He cleans you out and hits the road,
Then hurries home. His sleep is sound,
As the Good Book herein does propound.

The loot is in the villian's keeping,
But he can't enjoy it 'cause he's sleeping.
And you can't get to sleep in peace
With the whole house knee-deep in police.

But the Lord, in His mysterious ways,
Rewards the righteous man who prays:
Though Morpheus' arms will not immerse you,
Your insurance plan will reimburse you.

So that proverb may not be confusing
When it opts to deal with crime and snoozing.

Proverbs 6:6

[6]Go to the ant, thou sluggard;
Consider her ways and be wise; . . . (2)

Ant-thropology Sociology

The Good Book uses some psychology
And sheds new light on ant-thropology.
The ant, it seems, is always scurrying
And, apparently, does little worrying.

He, cleverly, has the potential
To make an anthill residential.
He lives well on a varied diet
With ample food but doesn't buy it.

Instead, with friends he rendezvous
At church bazaars, at barbecues
And picnics, at which his attendance
May explain his independence.

If he discovers food when browsin',
He invites another several thousand.
The ant, though filled with formic acid,
Is as generous as he is placid.

'Tis a pity for us that we can't,
Each one of us, be like that ant,
For sluggards would find life attractive
If, like the ants, they were more active.

If the ant were our adviser,
The Good Book says we'd all be wiser.

Proverbs 6:27-28

[27]Can a man take fire in his bosom
And his clothes not be burned?
[28]Or can one walk upon hot coals,
And his feet not be scorched? (2)

Cold Facts About a Hot Foot

In the Book of Proverbs, we have learned
If you play with fire, you can get burned.
That simple truth, one recognizes,
Appears in various disguises.

If one of your avowed goals
Is treading lightly on hot coals
And trusting you'll escape unsinged,
You've probably become unhinged.

Suppose your neighbor's wife you covet.
Although you're sure that she would love it,
You should recall those burning fires
And reconsider your desires.

If you're among the mischief-makers,
You won't be like those Hindu fakirs
Who, given somewhat to flamboyance,
Can walk on coals without annoyance.

So you should ponder as to whether
You think your feet are made of leather,
For in the Good Book, it's suggested
You're not fireproof, so don't be tested.

Proverbs 7:17-19

[17]I have perfumed my bed
With myrrh, aloes, and cinnamon.
[18]Come, let us take our fill of love until the morning;
Let us solace ourselves with loves.
[19]For my husband is not at home,
He is gone on a long journey; . . . (2)

Coma from the Aroma

Despite the good Book's pious phrasing,
It's apt to do some eyebrow raising
When it elects to be explicit
Regarding acts we'd deem illicit.

In Proverbs, there are exhortations
Condemning divers dissipations,
And in particular, it censures
Extramarital adventures.

The temptress who does the inviting
May make it all sound quite exciting;
However, don't be too ecstatic;
Reality may be traumatic.

Suppose in bed you were cavorting
As long as the Good Book's reporting,
And the temptress laced the atmosphere
With aloes, cinnamon and myrrh.

It's possible, from the aroma,
That you would wind up in a coma!
So your nose, the Good Book's words reveal,
Just might be your Achilles heel,

And in the end, from what's been stated,
You could end up asphyxiated.

So perhaps you should avoid such sirens
If they appear in your environs.

Proverbs 8:1, 10

[1]Doth not wisdom call,
And understanding put forth her voice?
[10]Receive my instruction, and not silver,
And knowledge rather than choice gold. (2)

Wisdom, Better Than Silver and Gold?

Regarding your net worth, you've Proverbs to thank
That for your chief assets you don't need a bank.
But if your spouse tells you that she'd like a necklace,
'Twould seem to be more than a little bit reckless
To make the suggestion that you'd rather get her
Something as precious which you think is better.

If your gift is wisdom instead of a pendant,
In a divorce court you'll be a defendant,
And although your wisdom may have many facets,
She will end up with the rest of your assets.

So you'd best use that wisdom to help you decide
Just where your priorities lay, re your bride.

Better than gold, to be well educated?
Still, it must be true if in Proverbs it's stated.

Proverbs 10:22

[22]The blessing of the Lord, it maketh rich,
And toil addeth nothing thereto. (2)

How to Join the Idle Rich

The Good Book says if we are pious
There's naught the Good Lord would deny us.
This proverb intimates He offers
To guarantee to fill our coffers
And lets us know that we can cash in
If we behave in faultless fashion.

If wealth's your goal and you'd pursue it,
Working overtime won't do it,
But when you're bad, I don't suppose He
Plans to make your path too rosy.
If His blessing you're forsaking,
All your assets He'll be taking.

Still, if you find that you recoil
From what is known as honest toil,
You need not feel that you are slacking,
Because your bankroll has His backing
As long as you find it expedient,
In all His ways, to be obedient.

Lie back, relax, be unafraid,
And the Good Book says you've got it made!

Proverbs 10:31

[31]The mouth of the righteous buddeth with wisdom;
But the froward tongue shall be cut off. (2)

The Righteous Man Zips His Lips

This proverb tells all to be wary
Whose tongues are froward and contrary.
Its threat is very clearly stated
If the language tends to be "X-rated."

The righteous will have the ability
To speak at all times with civility,
But if you should have the audacity
To sprinkle your words with mendacity,

Perhaps you should pause in your screeching
And give ear to the Good Book's teaching.
Be like the wise man who is copin':
His mouth is very rarely open.

Since the Good Book's words are not debatable,
And the tongue, it says, is amputatable,
If you're not careful when you speak,
You'll never speak with tongue in cheek.

Proverbs 11:1

[1]A false balance is an abomination to the Lord;
But a perfect weight is His delight. (2)

Keep Your Fingers off the Scales

In the Good Book, nothing is moroser
Than the thought of a dishonest grocer.
A one-pound weight the Lord denounces
If there are less than sixteen ounces;
He also disapproves those scams
Where the short weight is in kilograms.

Gas stations, too, are not immune.
A bolt of lightning could bring ruin
To owners practicing the arts
Of gallons having just three quarts —
Undoubtedly an indicator
That that's frowned upon by the Creator.

No amount of prayer prevails
If you keep your fingers on the scales.
There is no escape for one who cheats
When labeling prepackaged meats.
And in His Judgment Book, He jots
The owners of some used-car lots.

You must avoid all hocus-pocus
When on the bathroom scales you focus
Because the Lord makes no exceptions
For even such small self-deceptions.

So be wary of the Lord's displeasures,
For He oversees all weights and measures.

Proverbs 15:1

[1]A soft answer turneth away wrath; . . . (2)

A Soft Answer Turneth Away Wrath

Consider, briefly, this scenario:
Let's say that you're a gay Lothario
And certain wild thoughts you're instilling
In your best friend's wife, who's young and willing,

Then your friend arrives, some early a.m.,
With eyes a-blazing, bent on mayhem.
He rushes at you in high dudgeon,
Brandishing a fearsome bludgeon.

If you, in such a situation,
Should follow Proverbs' exhortation
And use the Good Book's well-known platitude
And employ soft words to change his attitude,

One thing that you may be discovering,
In Intensive Care, where you're recovering,
Is that gentle techniques of persuasion
Should be saved for just the right occasion.

~ Moral ~

There's a moral here for your survival:
When confronted by a vengeful rival —
On this point, there's no disagreeing —
There are times for soft words and for fleeing!

Proverbs 15:22

[22]For want of counsel purposes are frustrated;
But in the multitude of counsellors they are established. (2)

The "Why" of Three Branches of Government

The Good Book has a proverb
Which appears to be most fitting:
The quality of government
Depends on who is sitting
Within the sacred halls of state
To share with us their learning
And ponder such august events
As when they'll be adjourning.

It hints we can be led astray
By just one ignoramus,
But there is safety in a crowd
Whose motto is "don't blame us."
Our founding fathers weren't dumb;
They knew that proverb fully;
They made quite sure we'd not fall prey
To just one single bully.

They set up branches which they felt
Were ample and official:
The legislative, the exec,
And also the judicial.
Thus, when great issues make the rounds
Within those sacred portals,
They've made quite sure that they protect
Us ordinary mortals.

In each one of their great debates
They fasten on one item,
Which item begets others
And so on, ad infinitum,
For those discussions are productive
In the last analysis
Of legislative compromise
Or, worse, complete paralysis.

Thus, the Good Book here has made a point:
There's safety in large numbers;
Unhappily, though, most of them
All march to different drummers.

Proverbs 16:16

[16]How much better is it to get wisdom than gold!
Yea, to get understanding is rather to be chosen than silver. (2)

Yes, It Is Better Than Silver or Gold

It is written in Proverbs, so we are told,
That wisdom is better than silver or gold.
Still, it is quite likely no banker disburses
His bank's liquid assets based on some such verses.

Suppose I were hungry and one day, perchance,
I enter the caverns of higher finance.
I'd come face to face with the bank's chief director
And plead that he'd help ward off bankruptcy's specter.

I would ask that he lend, for a time, their resources,
On which he'd agree, but one rule he enforces —
A point which he felt that he should make with clarity:
His bank is a business house and not a charity,

And I must pledge assets so that there's no danger
That he might have, falsely, put faith in a stranger.

I'd assure him that faith need not be unilateral;
I'd just let my wisdom become my collateral.
But if, then, he seems less than philanthropistic,
There is no reason to be pessimistic,

For even though banks want more concrete security
And are disinclined to take wisdom as surety,
It's unlikely I'll be left out in the cold,
'Cause what I've got's better than silver or gold.

Yea, though I proclaim it at each opportunity,
It falls on deaf ears in the banking community.

Proverbs 16:18

[18]Pride goeth before destruction,
And a haughty spirit before a fall. (2)

Pride Goeth Before a Fall

The Book of Proverbs will provide
Some caveats regarding pride
And illustrates the true nobility
Of the lasting virtues of humility.

But I'm so very, very proud
The urge to shout that fact aloud
Is positively all-consumin'
Because I'm such a perfect human.

For adulation I am thirsting —
As you can see, I'm near to bursting —
And yet, in me, it's so becoming
That when you're near, I feel I'm slumming.

You mustn't view that as a slight
Because it's obvious I'm right.
It's plain that I need no rehearsin'
To be an almost perfect person.

And although tortured by the ghost
Of that little word "almost,"
I do not waste my time in sorrow,
For I'll be perfect by tomorrow.

It's unbecoming to show meekness.
Because it's clear I have no weakness,
The simple fact is, as I see it,
If I'm the greatest, then so be it.

Yet the Good Book says I must be humble,
A word on which most men would stumble,
But if I must, I'll show my worth —
I'LL BE THE HUMBLEST MAN ON EARTH!

Proverbs 17:18

[18]A man void of understanding is he that striketh hands,
And becometh surety in the presence of his neighbour. (2)

Get It in Writing, Notarized

In Proverbs, it hints you're some kind of a dummy —
And on this point, it gets no argument from me —
If your neighbor should ask that you cosign his note
And you just shake hands on what you underwrote.

Suppose that his creditors now make demands on it
And you, in your innocence, simply shook hands on it.
He's broke, and he's penniless — not misdemeanors,
But you'll be the one whom they take to the cleaners.

The lesson contained in this proverb is clear:
Though a handshake, as surety, may be sincere,
Instead of a handshake to prop up a debtor,
This proverb suggests that collateral's better.

Proverbs 17:28

[28]Even a fool, when he holdeth his peace, is counted wise;
And he that shutteth his lips is esteemed as a
man of understanding. (2)

Foot-in-Mouth Disease

The Good Book shows its perspicacity
Equating silence with sagacity.
So you can keep up the pretensions
Of having brains with great dimensions
If, when great issues are debated,
Your lips remain approximated.

If you can keep your gums from flappin',
Other good things also happen:
John Barleycorn will make no trips
Across a pair of padlocked lips,
And though an English trifle beckons,
You will never ask for seconds.

The loon, the dumbest of all birds,
Never has to eat his words,
So it's obvious your true salvation
Lies in avoiding conversation.

The Good Book urges, with tenacity,
That you should temper your loquacity,
And it guarantees you'll be respected
If your vocal cords are disconnected.

Proverbs 19:4

[4]Wealth addeth many friends;
But as for the poor, his friend separateth himself from him. (2)

The Poor Man Loses His Last Friend

The Good Book says, regarding amity,
That the recipe for a calamity
Is a pas de deux where one friend places
His friendship on a fiscal basis.

But friendships like ours have uniqueness,
For they're devoid of any weakness,
And though the world were going under,
Nothing could tear us asunder.

When you are skating on thin ice,
I'll be there with my advice,
And if it breaks and you fall through,
Count on me to rescue you.

If you are down and quite defenseless,
I won't let them beat you senseless,
And when your keepers come to get you,
I'll be right along to fetch you.

We'll carry on through life proclaimin'
That I'm your Pythias, you're my Damon.
All you need to do is holler,
And you can have my bottom dollar.

Although,

Way back there, when we were younger
And I was cold and weak from hunger,
You said, with wallet tightly folded,
"That's how character is molded."

And so don't think I love you any less
Just because you're down and penniless,
But when you're facing destitution,
You must show strength and resolution.

Although you'd hoped, in your duress,
That you could count on my largess,
Such thinking is just addle-pated
Because that's how friends are separated.

→

It's not that I am parsimonious,
But to give you cash would be erroneous.
It's time you showed you've got the guts
To pull yourself out of such ruts.
What I'm saying, and I hold no rancor,
Is, "Get lost, you bum. I'm not your banker!"

~ Moral ~

The Good Book leaves us with a warning,
A lesson one should not be scorning:
When the hand of friendship is extended,
If the palm is up, the friendship's ended!

Proverbs 19:24

24The sluggard buries his hand in the dish,
and will not even bring it back to his mouth. (1)

The Hand-in-the-Dish Syndrome

Though the tone of this proverb is blunt and declarative,
Its message is cloaked in a "hand-to-mouth" narrative
In which we are cautioned that sins such as sloth
Are wayward or wicked or, more likely, both,
But given the words of this proverb as stated,
Perhaps other meanings could be postulated.

Is it possible you would be somewhat ambivalent
If that dish contained gruel or, perhaps, its equivalent
And the sluggard, so-called, whom this proverb's abusing,
Let slip from his fingers the spoon he was using
And buried his hand in an effort prehensile
To grope in the gruel to retrieve that utensil?

Another idea with which we have been flirting:
Suppose that the hand were arthritic and hurting.
The doctors had proved to be less than omniscient,
And multiple nostrums had been inefficient,
And the dish's warm contents gave promise of healing . . .
Is that what the hand in the dish is revealing?

There are other meanings which could be as suitable:
The hand's in the dish — that one fact's indisputable.
If that hand were attached to a nearsighted person
Who thought it a finger bowl (so he's immersin'
The hand), would it not be at least understandable
That that hand would not pass from the dish to his mandible?

Though sloth is quite clearly this proverb's main topic,
To read it verbatim could just be myopic.
The reader may find the examples extreme.
Oftentimes things may not be what they seem.

~ Moral ~

If your neighbor seems lazy, and you just can't budge him,
Consider those options, and don't try to judge him.

Proverbs 20:1

[1]Wine is a mocker, strong drink is riotous;
And whosoever reeleth thereby is not wise. (2)

Strong Drink Is Riotous

The aim of the Good Book is that we should think
Before we succumb to the evils of drink.

"Oh, father, dear father, come home with me now
'Cause Mom's got arthritis and can't milk the cow;
The cow's udder's full, and it's liable to burst,
And me and the baby will perish from thirst.

"And, also, Mom told me to ask you to please
Return home this one time without the d.t.'s
'Cause when your hand trembles and tends to be fluttery,
The milk that emerges is more or less buttery.

"I can see, through those swinging doors, how you have sinned,
Stretched out on the floor and three sheets to the wind.
I'd help if I could 'cause you've ne'er been supiner,
But they won't let me in 'cause I'm only a minor."

So come home, repent and return to sobriety,
And ask for forgiveness and demonstrate piety.
You'll merit the Good Lord's forgiveness, albeit
The words of this proverb do not guarantee it.

But if you are foolin' and stay on the sauce,
You'll learn in a hurry just Who is the Boss.
Your punishment's sure to be proper and fitting,
For when dealing with tosspots, the Lord isn't kidding.

Proverbs 20:13

[13]Love not sleep, lest thou come to poverty;
Open thine eyes, and thou shalt have bread in plenty. (2)

No Apogees While Grabbing Zzzz

The Good Book has a proverb which is:
If you would be amassing riches
And choose the diamond, not the rhinestone,
Your nose must be kept to the grindstone;
You must keep sowing and keep reaping,
Which you can't do while you are sleeping.

If you'd be a financial climber,
You must possess a built-in timer
'Cause no one ever got ahead
By spending all his time in bed.

If Edison had slept long nights,
There would be no electric lights,
For if he'd stayed in bed, contented,
The light bulb would not be invented.

And if Marconi weren't tireless,
He'd never have thought up the wireless,
And the world would be less antiseptic
If Pasteur had been narcoleptic.

You aren't apt to do much earning
While you're tossing and you're turning,
For there is little one discovers
With his head beneath the covers
(Except for girls who make a bundle
Doing business in the trundle).

So don't wait for ideas to creep
Into your head while you're asleep,
For men don't reach their apogees
While they're recumbent, grabbing zzzz.

Thus, the Book of Proverbs' message links
Poverty with forty winks,
But for great riches, you won't lack
If you are an insomniac.

Proverbs 21:9

[9]It is better to dwell in a corner of the housetop,
Than in a house in common with a contentious woman. (2)

Ecstatic in the Attic

Proverbs, in this verse, reminds you
It's difficult to put behind you
The fact that you can't make revisions
To some of your unwise decisions.

Just possibly, you are embittered
By failing to have reconsidered
The step you took in haste toward wedlock,
Which, now, has got you in a headlock.

You might have been less acquiescent
If her nagging, which is now incessant,
Had been revealed by some clairvoyance
And spared you subsequent annoyance.

For had you been somewhat more tentative,
The fact that she was argumentative
May have persuaded you to falter
Along the pathway to the altar.

Your mansion has some eighty rooms in it,
Yet it's too small when her voice booms in it,
And though you built it to reside in it,
There's no safe place where you can hide in it.

Her vocalizing is stentorian,
And she uses words not mid-Victorian.
The walls, though solid, are no barrier,
And you ask yourself, "Why did I marry her?"

Though the thought of murder has some merit,
There's a simpler way, if you can bear it:
If you would like to be ecstatic,
Just move your things up to the attic,

Where, though you'll lack a few amenities,
You'll miss the bulk of her obscenities.
And no matter how loud she may screech, you
Will find her strident tones won't reach you.

The logic must be irrefutable
'Cause the Good Book says that method's suitable.

Proverbs 23:31-32

[31]Look not upon wine when it is red,
When it giveth its colour in the cup,
When it glideth down smoothly;
[32]At the last it biteth like a serpent,
And stingeth like a basilisk. (2)

Opt for Perrier Instead

This proverb frowns on wine that's red
And opts for Perrier instead,
For though "*in vino veritas*,"
That truth is often sad, alas.

Who mingles with the cognoscenti
In the world of spiritus frumenti
And spends each weekend fully "loaded"
Should read this proverb, for it's noted
That though the vineyard's grapes invite you,
Before you know it, they will bite you.

Be it Haut Brion or Manischewitz,
It's gall and wormwood that they have. It's
Just as true for fine champagne,
And this proverb tells you to abstain.

So junk the juice that makes you blotto.
That's the Book of Proverbs' motto.

Proverbs 28:1

[1]The wicked flee when no man pursueth; . . . (2)

The Wicked Flee When No Man Pursueth

Though joggers jog to maintain fitness,
This proverb tells us to bear witness
That wicked men who live by stealth
Are also running for their health.

It further hints that evildoers,
When fleeing from unseen pursuers,
Are oft inclined to look around
To see if someone's gaining ground.

So if in guilt you have been wallowing
And you imagine someone's following,
Don't feel that you'll avoid disaster
By speeding up and running faster

Because the Lord above will hound you;
He's not behind — He's all around you.
You can't avoid His wrath through cunning,
But mend your ways, and you'll stop running.

The Good Book, thusly, doth remind you
That you won't have to look behind you!

Proverbs 28:23

[23]He that rebuketh a man shall in the end find more favour
Than he that flattereth with the tongue. (2)

Your Guest Room Won't Be Overcrowded

Though not found in the Pentateuch,
Proverbs speaks about rebuke
And hints that, if you're so inclined,
'Twould add aught to your peace of mind
To read this proverb's verse and heed it
And tell your friends off when they need it.

He who flatters friends and neighbors
Garners nothing from his labors.
Rebukes, we're told, are more agreeable;
Results, though, may be unforeseeable.

When your best friend deserves reproach,
To offer same may be *très gauche*
Because if you're too blunt with friends,
The friendship, in most cases, ends.

And for your honesty and candor
You just might wind up sued for slander.
One thing is true, no doubt about it:
Your guest room won't be overcrowded.

Proverbs 30:18-19

[18]There are three things which are too wonderful for me,
Yea, four which I know not:
[19]The way of an eagle in the air;
The way of a serpent upon a rock;
The way of a ship in the midst of the sea;
And the way of a man with a young woman. (2)

The Age-Old Battle of the Sexes

The Good Book tends to be quite serious
In contemplating the mysterious.
Four things too wonderful to fathom
Are spelled out, and this proverb hath 'em.

Wise men have learned the why and wherefore
Of ancient puzzlements, and, therefore,
We know just how the eagle glided
Across the skies before United
And understand their aerobatics
By using basic mathematics,
For they could stay up in the heavens
Before the Lockheed 1011s.

The ancient scholars had no notion
Of the serpent's means of locomotion,
And they viewed his wondrous undulation
With uncompromising fascination.
He slithers forward on his belly
As if his spine were made of jelly,
But his vertebrae are the key factors
According to most chiropractors.

A source of ancient controversy
Was sailing at the weather's mercy.
Each ship sailed where the trade winds blew it,
And if it foundered, no one knew it.
Today, large vessels move commuters
Across the ocean by computers,
Yet praying still has its adherents
When hurricanes make their appearance.

But the age-old battle of the sexes,
Today, continues to perplex us.
We learn, from reading ancient history,
*

That the ways of love were then a mystery.
The rites of lovers reached fruition
By using simple intuition,
But the path by which true love has traveled
The Good Book's words have not unravelled.

It's said love springs from Cupid's dart,
But hormones must have played a part.

Proverbs 30:28

[28]The spider thou canst take with the hands,
Yet is she in kings' palaces. (2)

The Spider and the Fly

The spider was engaged
In conversation with the fly.
He said, "I much prefer my fate,
And here's the reason why:
It's true I can be trapped within
The palm of either hand,
And why I make most ladies shriek,
I cannot understand."

"That doesn't sound so great to me,"
The housefly interjected.
"I'm free and soar just like a bird,
Although I'm less respected."

The spider then replied, "Although
I can't fly like an eagle,
My chosen habitat is often
Nothing less than regal.
I'm quite at home in every crevice
In a royal castle
And not despised nor spat upon
As if I were a vassal.

"It should be crystal clear to even
You, my flying friend,
That though I could be stepped upon,
I win out in the end.
To you, friend fly, a meaner fate
Has ever been allotted
'Cause you must spend most of your life
Avoiding being swatted."

This proverb seems to tell us that
Despite the spider's size,
He lives the life of Riley
Just by dint of being wise.
And you, the reader, although small,
Can likewise be successful,
Though living like the spider does
Is apt to be quite stressful.

Proverbs 31:10

[10]A woman of valour who can find?
For her price is far above rubies. (2)

A Woman of Valor, Who Can Find?

"A virtuous girl is hard to find"
Is what the Good book had in mind,
But Proverbs on thin ice is skating
When jewels and women it's equating.

If you aspire to keep housebound
That jewel you've already found,
You must expend much of your treasure,
Though it may give you little pleasure,
For if she fills the bill, she merits
A diamond weighing several carats.

If you're too cheap for such a bauble,
You could be in a heap of trauble,
For no man should be so penurious
As not to opt for the luxurious.

And though a rhinestone might just hurt you less,
Your jewel of jewels could wind up virtueless!

Job 1:1

[1]There was a man in the land of Uz, whose name was Job; and that man was whole-hearted and upright, and one that feared God, and shunned evil. (2)

A Good Man, Job, and His Travail

The Good Book tells a sorry tale
Of a good man, Job, and his travail.
A man of wealth and great possessions,
He was free of sin and all transgressions.
He trod the narrow path of virtue.
If you're good, he reasoned, naught can hurt you.

Job didn't lie, steal or philander.
He was an innocent bystander
Unwittingly participatin'
In a wager 'twixt the Lord and Satan.

Said Satan, "Job is not perfection.
I can make him lean in my direction.
If he should suffer great privation,
He'll spurn You without hesitation."

So the Devil pulled out all the stops.
He killed Job's flocks and burned his crops.
Then, just as Satan had predicted,
With hideous sores Job was afflicted.

But Job's heart really started achin'
When his sons and daughters all were taken
And his wife was bordering on insanity.
Yet, somehow, Job eschewed profanity.

And Satan stood there flabbergasted
'Cause all Job did was prayed and fasted,
But an end came to Job's impassivity,
And he cursed the day of his nativity.

In the end, however, Job repented,
And the Good Lord, on His part, relented.
So Job was blessed with ten descendants
And restored to fiscal independence.

Though Job was nigh unto perfection,
He was the victim, on reflection.
His entire world so torn asunder.
Why? It kinda makes you wonder.

By extrapolation, it's suggested
If you're not pure, you won't be tested!

Job 37:14-15

[14]Hearken unto this, O Job;
Stand still, and consider the wondrous works of God.
[15]Dost thou know how God enjoineth them,
And causeth the lightning of His cloud to shine? (2)

Job in New York City?

Though the Book of Job is ancient history,
Some questions still remain a mystery.

Would patience melt into self-pity
If he had lived in New York City?
Instead of losing all his flocks,
Would he just fret about his stocks
And wonder how he'd overcome it
If the Dow Jones average were to plummet?

I'm confident Job would be nervous
If confronted with our Postal Service,
And he'd have cursed each home appliance
On which he'd come to place reliance
When learning that, for each, the essence
Was very short-term obsolescence.

Would chasing taxies, in the end,
Nudge our hero "'round the bend"
Or when he'd found a place for parking
And learned, alas, on disembarking,
He had no coins to feed the meter?
Would patience still prevail, dear reader?

In the Good Book, Job put up with suffering
With neither compromise nor buffering
And gained therefrom much notoriety
For his faith and for his piety.
Could Job have held on to that piety
Living in today's society?

But the Good Book says Job was unflappable,
So he'd have made the grade in the Big Appable.

Song of Solomon 1:1-2

[1]The Song of Songs, which is Solomon's.
[2]O that you would kiss me with the kisses of your mouth!
For your love is better than wine, . . . (1)

She Was the Only Ethiopian

The Song of Songs, far from pedantic,
Is sizzling hot; it's so romantic,
A sort of how-to-do-it text
Designed to please the oversexed.
As was the rule in that society,
Solomon's tastes ran to variety.

In chapter one, he has a choice.
"I am dark and comely," says a voice.
The Queen of Sheba, far from meek,
Was advertising, so to speak,
Her wares, for in Sol's world utopian,
She was the only Ethiopian.

When the Good Book's read in Alabama,
They all give wide berth to that drama,
And their attitude is rather glacial
Because the Song of Songs is interracial.

So the Good Book has at times reflected
Touches of the unexpected!

Song of Solomon 4:1, 7:3

[1]Behold, thou art fair, my love; behold, thou art fair;
Thine eyes are as doves behind thy veil; . . .
[3] . . . Thy belly is like a heap of wheat . . . (2)

Each Leg an Alabaster Column

The Song of Songs, though not X-rated,
Is, in some ways, unexpurgated
Since it is certain to elicit
Behavior more or less explicit.

It's laced with metaphors so torrid
That beads of sweat bedeck your forehead
As it dawns on you that such quotations
Could help your marital relations.

The very least of lovers drools
At "rounded thighs that are like jewels,"
And it's not easy staying solemn
With each leg "an alabaster column."

She's said to be the "rose of Sharon";
Her beauty is beyond comparin';
Her cheeks are like a "bed of spices,"
And lips hint at what Paradise is.

Breasts, we read, are "breasts like fawns,"
And skin the finest of chiffons.
With a profile that is classic Grecian,
Passion is what she's unleashin',

But what causes one to lose control
Is "a navel like a rounded bowl,"
Plus "a belly like a heap of wheat" —
In short, she's good enough to eat.

The Song of Songs no doubt explores
Some rather far-fetched metaphors,
But you get the message, though it's flowery:
Girls are made with a built-in dowry.

Ruth 1:16-17

[16]But Ruth said, "Entreat me not to leave you or to return from following you; for where you go I will go, and where you lodge I will lodge; your people shall be my people, and your God my God; [17]where you die I will die, and there will I be buried. . . ." (1)

The World Champion Daughter-in-Law

The Book of Ruth should give us pause
To meditate on mother-in-laws.
Ruth and Naomi, for example,
Give testimony more than ample
That one should not, in haste, disparage
A mother and daughter linked by marriage.

Ruth rang the doorbell of Naomi
And said, "I'm Ruth; I guess you know me."
"Of course, of course, come in the house.
You're my daughter-in-law, my late son's spouse."
And when she asked Ruth what her plans were,
From Ruth's lips came that famous answer:

"Whither thou goest, there go I.
Where thou liest, I'm nearby.
Where thy head rests, I'll put mine.
When thou borrowest, I'll cosign.
Whatever course you may pursue,
I'll stick with you like Elmer's glue.

"Through thick and thin, flu and bronchitis,
Nobody can subdivide us.
Though we're not of the same persuasion,
Nonetheless, we're both Caucasian.
Your people likewise I'll adopt.
That's the destiny for which I opt."

Said Naomi, "Well, that's very nice.
I appreciate the sacrifice,
But since I'm old and less alluring,
Let's opt for something more enduring,
A course of action indisputable,
Like a husband whom you would find suitable."

And the Good Book tells about her plan
To find Ruth a nice Jewish man.

Ruth 2:8, 14, 3:7

[8]Then Boaz said to Ruth, "Now, listen, my daughter, do not go to glean in another field . . . but keep close to my maidens."

[14]And at mealtime Boaz said to her, "Come here, and eat some bread, and dip your morsel in the wine." . . .

[7] . . . Then she came softly, and uncovered his feet, and lay down. (1)

The World Champion Mother-in-Law

This is Part Two, which part reveals
Just how Naomi "wheels and deals."
To the nearby fields she sent Ruth so as
To catch the eye of her kinsman Boaz.
He took one look at young Ruth's figure;
His eyes grew big and then grew bigger.

He said, "May I help with your gleaning
In my gazebo . . . if you take my meaning?"
Now, Ruth of Moab was no stranger
To such inducements and their danger
Because she'd known such invites
From young and lusty Moabites.

So she gathered up her skirts and fled . . .
At least, that's what the Good Book said.
But Naomi sighed, "Look, he's related,
So what if you capitulated?"
And she hustled Ruth back, *tout de suite*,
To spend the night at Boaz's feet.

Now, that's, of course, the Good Book's version
About that overnight excursion.
It must be plain, if you're a skeptic,
That version's somewhat antiseptic,
So use your own imagination
About Ruth's method of persuasion.

Naomi went to work with zeal
And said, "Boaz, let's make a deal."
Boaz would buy the real estate
Of Naomi's dear departed mate,
And, in the world of business jargon,
She threw in Ruth to seal the bargain.

So Ruth was wed, not once but twice,
On her mother-in-law's advice,
And each one got a proper share:
Naomi rich; Boaz an heir.
And that's how Ruth, as you'll discover,
Became King David's great-grandmother.

That's what took place in the Book of Ruth,
And the Good Book always tells the truth.

Ecclesiastes 1:1-5

[1]The words of the Preacher, the son of David, king in Jerusalem.
[2]Vanity of vanities, says the Preacher, vanity of vanities! All is vanity.
[3]What does man gain by all the toil at which he toils under the sun?
[4]A generation goes, and a generation comes,
but the earth remains for ever.
[5]The sun rises and the sun goes down,
and hastens to the place where it rises. (1)

Vanity of Vanities; All Is Vanity

When the sun disappears, that is not cause for sorrow.
We know that, for sure, it will come up tomorrow.
All things that seem new are, in truth, an illusion,
For they've happened before; that's the Good Book's
conclusion.

Rich man or poor man, the Preacher reminds us,
The same hand of fate, in the end, always finds us,
So the quest for great wealth is no more than quixotic,
And to die with your bank account full . . . idiotic!

The struggle for affluence challenges sanity.
All things come full circle . . . in the end, all is vanity,
Don't husband your fortune. He is thrice blessed who spends it.
That's what we should do. The Good Book recommends it!

Ecclesiastes 1:9

[9]What has been is what will be, and what has been done is what will be done; and there is nothing new under the sun. (1)

And There Is Nothing New Under the Sun

The Good Book, writ in days of yore,
Says everything's been done before.
But if those writers were more current,
Would they believe that all things weren't?

Would those sages be distraught
By the changes time has wrought?
Would their eyes pop, inasmuch as
They'd see sundry items such as

Trash compacters in the kitchen,
Antihistamines for itchin',
Films developed while you're waiting,
Worldwide overpopulating,

Aerosol cans if you're shaving,
All devices labor-saving,
Satellite communications,
Religion-only TV stations,

Warmup suits and nylon jackets,
Oversized Prince tennis racquets,
Ice cubes, half-moon shaped or cubic,
Puzzles with strange names like "Rubik,"

Oriental firms like Sony,
Turkey meat found in baloney,
TV games with monstrous prizes,
Ready-made clothes in odd sizes,

Computers found in third-grade classes,
A whole new concept of what "grass" is,
And weather news and low-cal brews
And Reebok shoes in rainbow hues?

But the Good Book's a respected teacher,
And the son of David (he's the preacher)
Tells us that there's nothing new;
Therefore, I guess, it must be true.

Ecclesiastes 2:18-19, 24

[18]I hated all my toil in which I had toiled under the sun, seeing that I must leave it to the man who will come after me; [19]and who knows whether he will be a wise man or a fool? . . .

[24]There is nothing better for a man than that he should eat and drink, and find enjoyment in his toil. This also, I saw, is from the hand of God; . . . (1)

The IRS Will Get It, Surely

The Good Book aims to reassure us,
In words right out of Epicurus,
That living well, with nothing lacking,
Is apt to have the Good Lord's backing.

Those words are set forth to remind you
Not to leave your wealth behind you,
For if you pop off prematurely,
The IRS will get it, surely.

If you incline toward criticism
Of verses that preach hedonism,
Your life could stand some reassessing,
And this chapter may well be a blessing.

So enjoy your work and its rewards
'Cause you never know what's in the cards,
And spend what you've accumulated.
In this chapter, that's what's advocated.

Ecclesiastes 3:1-2, 4

[1]To every thing there is a season, and a time to every purpose under the heaven:
[2]A time to be born, and a time to die; A time to plant, and a time to pluck up that which is planted; . . .
. . . [4]A time to weep, and a time to laugh; . . . (2)

Are You in the Lord's Computer?

With these words, matchless in their beauty,
The Ecclesiast has done his duty,
Though the essence of his masterpiece is
Fatalistic in its thesis.

Enjoy your days and be convivial.
Don't worry over matters trivial,
For, as these verses have explained,
Your span of life is foreordained.

Take chances; be not conscience-smitten.
Your ending has long since been written.
Though you be saint or alms-box looter,
Your name's there in the Lord's computer.

* * *

But one thought enters at this junction:
If His computer should malfunction,
There's nothing you can do to change it.
How will the Good Lord rearrange it?

Suppose you're A, another B,
Some angel presses the wrong key!
Now, countless evils B has wrought,
But B is spared, and you are not.

Should you conclude you've been forsaken,
Now that the place of B you've taken?
Will B be spared that one-way trip
Due to an errant microchip?

Will there be angels shedding tears
High in the celestial spheres
Since due to faults in their endeavor,
B could stay on earth forever?

But for all things there is a season,
And though B might not find it pleasin',
He'll pay his debts, there's no escape,
'Cause the Good Lord has a backup tape.

Ecclesiastes 5:9-10

[9]A lover of money never has his fill of money, nor a lover of wealth his fill of income. That too is futile. [10]As his substance increases, so do those who consume it; . . . (3)

Their Hands Are in Your Pockets

If you have wealth and you're not hiding it,
You'll have scores of folks dividing it:
Some to brokers, some to lawyers,
Some withheld by your employers.

Accountants get theirs by osmosis,
Keeping track of what your gross is,
And countless others on the docket
With one or both hands in your pocket.

Groups of every ilk will hound you
In numbers that will quite astound you,
But till you're verging on the penniless,
Most of them won't hound you any less.

Although your greed remains untiring,
Someone is out there conspiring,
In subtle ways, to take your measure
And separate you from your treasure.

No need to worry where to send it —
Lots of friends will help you spend it.
You'll get ulcers from collecting it
And nervous breakdowns from protecting it.

So heed the words, here, of the Preacher:
Though you're an avaricious creature
And have a talent for great riches,
They'll clean you out, those . . . friends who love you.

Ecclesiastes 7:10

[10]*Say not, "Why were the former days better than these?"* . . . (1)

The Good Old Days

The Good Book doesn't lavish praise
On what folks call "the good old days."

To oldsters, those years seem much nearer
When viewed through their rear-vision mirror.
They see all things, as more time passes,
Through what we'd call "rose-colored glasses":

"We had no crime; the streets were spotless.
The kids learned more, and they forgot less.
Milk was bottled, not in cartons.
There weren't any Dolly Partons.

"No high-priced spas for weight reduction,
No atom bombs for mass destruction,
Silent movies, no profanity,
No packaged TV Christianity."

A litany of bygone purity,
A grieving for long-lost security,
But we're told by the Ecclesiastic,
"Let's not be too enthusiastic.

"For days gone by, be not enraptured;
The past can never be recaptured."
So I guess from now on I shall frown on it
'Cause the Good Book, here, has turned thumbs down on it.

Ecclesiastes 11:9-10

[9]O Youth, enjoy yourself while you are young! . . . Follow the desires of your heart and the glances of your eyes — but know well that God will call you to account for all such things [10] — and banish care from your mind, . . . For youth and black hair are fleeting. (3)

Gather Ye Rosebuds While Ye May

The Good Book says the time to cash in
On your ardor and your passion
Is when you're handsome, young and dashin',
Before your hair has turned to ashen.

But at some things the Good Book's balking,
So when you're on the prowl and stalking
The blond with whom you have been talking,
You'd better do some tightrope walking.

She may be shapely, young and willing,
And you think you can make a killing.
Although you find the prospect thrilling,
The Good Book's caveats are chilling.

They warn you: though she be alluring,
Some actions you should be abjuring,
For it is less than reassuring
That some diseases are enduring.

And so, beware of those excesses,
Even if she acquiesces.
There'll be no need for second guesses
If you don't catch what she possesses.

That said . . .

Lest you exaggerate your fears,
The Good Book to this thought adheres:
The joy of youth soon disappears,
So don't neglect your salad years.

Ecclesiastes 12:12

[12] . . . Of making many books, there is no end, and much study is a weariness of the flesh. (1)

Of Making Books, There Is No End

There are too many books in print —
The Good Book tells us so,
And it came to that conclusion
Some two thousand years ago.

And yet, within each person
There's a book that is just yearning
To catch the public's fancy
And embellish what one's earning.

But before you catch the fancy
Of the public and its dollars,
You'll have to run the gauntlet
Of both publishers and scholars.

The scholars will determine
If your brainchild comes full flower,
But the former, the book publishers,
Possess the veto power.

Although, perhaps, you're wont to say,
"No book's as good as mine is,"
The publisher will want to know
Just what the bottom line is.

But do not be discouraged
Though you've nothing but rejections;
Your book could see the light of day
Despite its imperfections.

Of making books, there is no end,
But that need not concern you.
If your ms. has gore and sex,
The publishers won't spurn you.

Esther 2:16-17

[16] So Esther was taken unto king Ahasuerus into his house royal in the tenth month, which is the month of Tebeth, in the seventh year of his reign. [17]And the king loved Esther above all the women, and she obtained grace and favour in his sight more than all the virgins; so that he set the royal crown upon her head, and made her queen instead of Vashti. (2)

Soap Opera, Part I: Heroine

The Book of Esther tells of royalty
And of Esther's steadfast Hebrew loyalty.

In Esther's story is depicted
A queen who has just been evicted.
The heroine is her successor.
There's a villain who is an oppressor;
There's a hero, honest and God-fearing,
Who wins out 'cause he's persevering.
Intrigue and love and tensions blending —
Result, of course, a happy ending.
(With a few good tenor ariettas,
It would sound like Lehar's operettas.)

The queen was Vashti, who resisted
Commands on which the king insisted.
The good king, having thus erased her,
Held a contest and replaced her,
And according to an old tradition,
Each candidate had one audition.

Of course, the Bible does not mention
How Esther got the king's attention,
For the Good Book uses great discretion
In reporting on the royal succession,
But the fact is that when they awakened,
The position was no longer vacant.

And Esther won the royal scepter;
Apparently, she'd been adepter.

Esther 2:7

[7]And he brought up Hadassah, that is, Esther, his uncle's daughter; for she had neither father nor mother, and the maiden was of beautiful form and fair to look on; and when her father and mother were dead, Mordecai took her for his own daughter. (2)

Soap Opera, Part II: Hero

Queen Esther had a foster parent
Named Mordecai, who was adherent
To the Hebrew faith that he was born in,
And at the palace gate one mornin'
To gather news about his daughter,
He heard men plot the monarch's slaughter.
He foiled the plot; it was avoided
(And the plotters promptly eunuchoided).
He acted thusly, never dreaming
'Twas a marker he'd soon be redeeming.

* * *

The name of Haman casts a chill on us.
'Mongst villains, he was the most villainous.
He twirled his mustache, wore one earring,
And his enemies kept disappearing.
People lived in mortal terror
Lest they should make one little error.
Never had a king's prime minister
Been so arrogant and sinister.

But Mordecai, it is related,
Refused to be intimidated,
And that caused Haman to be furious.
He hatched a scheme that was injurious
To every Hebrew in the nation —
We're talking mass annihilation —
And he built a gallows with a noose
For Mordecai's exclusive use.

As the reader soon surmises,
One noose fits all collar sizes,
And the bad guy's days were growing short
'Cause the good guys had the Lord's support.

Esther 7:1-2, 6

[1]So the king and Haman came to the banquet with Esther the queen. [2]And the king said again unto Esther on the second day at the banquet of wine: 'Whatever thy petition, queen Esther, it shall be granted thee; . . .'

[6] . . . Then Haman was terrified before the king and queen. (2)

Soap Opera, Part III: Villain

The Book of Esther, as is proper,
Tells how Haman came a cropper:
He had to have the king's permission
For his evil plans to reach fruition.
Though Haman got the royal ring
To seal the orders of the king,
The orders were so slow in traveling
That Haman's plot began unravelling.

To begin with, he had not foreseen
That a Jewess was, in fact, his queen.
Learning of her people's plight,
She gave a banquet that same night.
The only guest, of course, was Haman,
At whose undoing she was aimin'.

It's clear the fat was in the fire
When Haman started to perspire
'Cause the king, reminded by his wife
That Mordecai once saved his life,
Said, "Gosh, that's just an oversight,
Which I can rectify tonight.
What's proper and what should suffice is
One of Haman's own devices."

The queen knew that he was a goner
When Haman threw himself upon her
And begged her, would it be convenient
For her to be a trifle lenient?

When the king saw Haman prone on Esther,
He said, "Look here, Haman, you're a guest here,
And you're doing something I prohibit,
So you'll hang, forthwith, from your own gibbet."

And Mordecai, just hours later,
Was the king's new Chief Administrator.

That tale, some say, is an invention,
But it certainly held your attention,
And the Good Book's done its duty, viz.:
To tell the story like it is.

Daniel 2:48, 3:26

[48]Then the king made Daniel great, . . . and made him to rule over the whole province of Babylon, . . .

[26] . . . Then Shadrach, Meshach and Abed-nego, came forth out of the midst of the fire. (2)

No Fuel like an Old Fuel

When Dan became the country's master,
Things began to happen faster.
The king was fond of his Judeans,
Which seemed to upset the plebeians.

They said, "No Jews will overturn us"
And threw them in a fiery furnace,
But the Jews sat there in fiery splendor
Without becoming one bit tender.

They smiled and said, "Though you detest us,
Our clothes, you see, are all asbestos,
And we're not even slightly toasted,"
But the villains nearly wound up roasted.

You may think no tale could be phonier,
But it impressed the folks in Bablyonier.

Daniel 5:24-25

. . . [24]then was the palm of the hand sent from before Him, and this writing was inscribed. [25]And this is the writing that was inscribed: MENE MENE, TEKEL UPHARSIN. (2)

Mene, Mene, Tekel, Upharsin

Nebuchadnezzar disappears
And leaves a son of tender years.

The new king, yclept Belshazzar
(Not Dan; his name is Belteshazzar),
Set out to rid, by devious means,
All Babylon of the Judeans.

He gave a feast and served champagne
In goblets that were once Judean.
The Judeans thought, "That's blasphemous
To use that stolen glass from us."

In a flash, the king beheld the scrawl
Of a ghostly hand upon the wall,
And Belshazzar was terror-smitten
By what the ghostly hand had written:

"*Mene, Mene, Tekel, Upharsin*,"*
Four words of cryptic origin.
His wise men did not know who wrote it.
King Belshazzar could not decode it,

And Belteshazzar's interpretation
Brought Belshazzar great consternation.
Said Dan, "The Lord says you've been fired!"
And that same night, the king expired,

And Babylon, in the Good Book's versions,
Was conquered by the Medes and Persians.

---

*Recent scholarly biblical research has uncovered the surprising fact that this apparent neologism is actually an Aramaic transliteration of the ancient Confucian law of the inevitability of consequences: "Many, many tickle — you force grin" became "*Mene, mene, tekel, upharsin*."

Daniel 6:17-18

[17]Then the king commanded, and they brought Daniel, and cast him into the den of lions. Now the king spoke and said unto Daniel: 'Thy God whom thou servest continually, He will deliver thee.' [18]And a stone was brought, and laid upon the mouth of the den; and the king sealed it with his own signet, and with the signet of his lords; that nothing might be changed concerning Daniel. (2)

Daniel Won't Take It Lion Down

The Good Book tells of Daniel's deeds
Among the Persians and the Medes.
Though Darius Rex befriended Daniel,
His enemies produced a manual
And found a rule forbidding prayers
To any god that wasn't theirs.

They hatched a plan that was nefarious,
Which they presented to King Darius.
Now, Daniel was, in fact, uncritical
Of machinations so political,
So he scarcely raised an eyebrow when
They tossed him in the lions' den.

He simply stood there in defiance,
Which more or less surprised the lionce.
Before long, Darius detected
Things weren't going as expected.
The king, in order to save face,
Had Daniel's enemies take his place,
And from their fate, there were some signs
That the Good Lord also speaks to lions.

Those are the actual facts, I warrant,
Though some of you may think they aren't,
But I'd not wish to cast aspersions
On any of the Good Book's versions.

Ezra 1:1-2

[1]Now in the first year of Cyrus king of Persia, that the word of the Lord by the mouth of Jeremiah might be accomplished, the Lord stirred up the spirit of Cyrus king of Persia, that he made a proclamation throughout all his kingdom, and put also in writing, saying: [2]'. . . and He hath charged me to build Him a house in Jerusalem, which is in Judah.' (2)

Cyrus' Papyrus

When the Temple was destroyed,
The Hebrew people were annoyed,
But there wasn't much that they could do about it.
By the time the deed was done,
They were slaves in Babylon.
By Nebuchadnezzar's legions they'd been routed.

Though it was a monstrous crime,
They just said, "Let's bide our time;
Those Babylonians will rue their evil deeds."
And Ezra in this verse recites
How Cyrus helped the Israelites —
That's Cyrus, king of Persians and the Medes.

King Cyrus said, "Okay,
You are free as of today.
It's time you laid your synagogue's foundation.
You're forty thousand strong,
So go back where you belong.
I hereby make this royal proclamation."

Said the Jews, "We're not naive —
You could have aces up your sleeve,
So put your words in writing, please, King Cyrus.
You said we're free — okay, so be it!
But we'll believe it when we see it.
Just put that royal decree on a papyrus."

"That's no sooner said than done,"
Cyrus said. "I've just begun.
I'll also lend you cash to get you started.
We're God-fearing people here,
But it's your God that we fear.
Yes, we fear His awesome wrath when you've departed.

→

"Although we have our own gods,
We'd like to even up the odds,
So I'll handle all the financing that's needed.
If you'll just say a prayer for Cyrus,
Who initialed that papyrus,
When your reconstruction project is completed."

At the end of Cyrus' years,
Artaxerxes' name appears
(He's the next king in the royal house succession).
When the work came to a halt,
It was Artaxerxes fault.
To hold on to the Jews was his obsession.

But the Jews finessed that caper.
They said, "Go read Cyrus' paper,"
A suggestion that the Persian monarch heeded.
"Omigosh, that's what's decreed,
So I'll supply the funds you need."
And in the end, the Temple was completed.

As these chronicles attest,
Things just worked out for the best.
The Persians made no effort to bamboozle 'em.
The Good Lord's Temple was rebuilt
With no blood in anger spilt.
And that's how the Jews resettled in Jerusalem.

I Chronicles 11:22-23

[22]And Benaiah the son of Jehoiada was a valiant man of Kabzeel, a doer of great deeds; . . . [23]And he slew an Egyptian, a man of great stature, five cubits tall. The Egyptian had in his hand a spear like a weaver's beam; but Benaiah went down to him with a staff, and snatched the spear out of the Egyptian's hand, and slew him with his own spear. (1)

Benaiah Takes on Wilt the Stilt

One mighty chieftain called Benaiah
Was five feet tall, not one inch higher,
But despite his short and stocky figure,
He battled foes who were much bigger.

In one fight, which could not be gorier,
He took on an Egyptian warrior
Five cubits tall,* a walking tower
Before whom lesser men would cower.

He took aim at the tall man's head
And hit him in the groin instead.
The Egyptian doubled up, exclaiming,
"You didn't hit where you were aiming!"

Then Benaiah swung and deftly dealt
Another blow below the belt.
His foe, thus smitten, screamed in terror
And loosed his spear — a fatal error.

B. quickly grasped the situation:
"With that spear, I'll end this altercation."
He aimed, and what do you suppose?
One tall Egyptian — adios!

So the Good Book tells us, blow by blow,
Just how it happened long ago.

---

*One cubit, linear, dear readers,
Is o-point-four-five-seven meters.
How tall is that? Well, were he slender,
He'd be the Boston Celtics' center.
At any rate, from that description,
He was one very tall Egyptian.

I Chronicles 18:1-3

[1] . . . David smote the Philistines, and subdued them, and took Gath and its towns out of the hand of the Philistines. [2]And he smote Moab; and the Moabites became servants to David, and brought presents. [3]And David smote Hadarezer king of Zobah by Hamath, . . . (2)

What Happened to That Sweet Boy David?

In Chronicles, you can take note
Of all those whom King David smote,
For David had a yen to smite
Almost everyone in sight.
At smiting foes both near and far,
He was the undisputed czar.

How often have I wished to be
More like David, less like me,
No Caspar Milquetoast but much bolder,
With a chip perched on my shoulder.

I'd smite each neighbor in my sector
Who's young or thin or stands erecter.
I'd smite all those engaged in sports
Who look good in their tennis shorts.

I'd smite my income tax adviser
And every up-at-dawn ariser,
The guy ahead of me in line,
The one whose shoes have mirror shine.

What's more, I'm sure I'd like to smite
Anyone more erudite.
I'd smite my dentist, without qualms.
I'd smite all those with itchy palms,

And there are more I'd like to smite:
Those excessively polite,
Those who phone me during dinner
And every single lottery winner.

I'd smite those with temerity
To try to disagree with me
And wreak great havoc and disorder
On those high in the pecking order.

But I'm no David as a smiter.
At the sight of blood, I just turn whiter.
Unhappily, I'm just plain me,
But I have lots of company.

The Lord, I'm sure, said, "Let there be
Less like David, more like me."
For if there were Davids by the millions,
Soon there would be no civilians.

I Chronicles 19:1-2, 4

[1]And it came to pass after this, that Nahash the king of the children of Ammon died, and his son reigned in his stead.
[2] . . . So David sent messengers to comfort him concerning his father. . . .

[4]So Hanun took David's servants, and shaved them, and cut off their garments in the middle, even to their hips, . . . (2)

The Issue, in the End, Was Skirted

When Nahash, King of Ammon, perished,
So did the friendship David cherished.
When David sent a delegation
As mourners for the Hebrew nation,
The new king, who was paranoid,
Was something less than overjoyed.

King Hanun sneered, "That's not remorse.
Those guys are just a Trojan horse."
King David's envoys, who were mourning,
Were taken captive without warning,
And each was flaunted with impunity
Before the Ammonite community.

Hanun made those envoys furious.
He cut their beards, which were luxurious,
And to make sure that they'd been disgraced,
Their skirts were cut off at the waist.

When the envoys were thus ventilated,
The Ammonites were fascinated.
They gaped and snickered in derision
'Cause they'd never seen a circumcision,
And they wondered how an entire nation
Could undergo such amputation.

Said David, "Hanun, it was crude
To leave my envoys semi-nude.
We don't take lightly, in our nation,
Your Ammonite humiliation."

What started with a pair of shears
Was settled using swords and spears,
And every Hebrew did his duty,
The usual outcome: tons of booty,
So much stuff that, for them to carry it,
They had to use Hertz Rent-a-Chariot.

Though with soft porn the Good Book flirted,
The issue, in the end, was skirted.
But for Hanun's ploy ecdysiastic,
His punishment was rather drastic.

II Chronicles 1:17

[17]They imported a chariot from Egypt for six hundred shekels of silver, and a horse for a hundred and fifty; likewise through them these were exported to all the kings of the Hittites and the kings of Syria. (1)

Solomon's Import-Export Business

Attention, Kmart shoppers!

Our executives have MBA's from places such as Wharton.
We think our operation's mean and lean.
We try to keep our prices low — in fact, they're even spartan —
But there are measures we have not foreseen.

Though we know our Dun & Bradstreet and our Forbes, it's not surprising —
And we think it's more than just a bit ironical —
That there are other lessons to be learned in merchandising,
Which show up in the second book of Chronicles.

King Solomon, we learned, just dealt in chariots and horses,
But he made a fast buck with a small investment.
We didn't study Solomon in any of our courses,
But we've learned a few things reading the Old Testament.

So, attention, Kmart shoppers! Here, you'll get rock-bottom prices.
No, we're not the Casbah! Yet it seems to strike us
That we've used the Good Book's lessons, and we've made great sacrifices,
So give Solomon the credit if you like us.

II Chronicles 2:1-2, 5:6, 7:5

[1]Now Solomon purposed to build a temple for the name of the Lord, and a royal palace for himself. [2]And Solomon assigned seventy thousand men to bear burdens and eighty thousand to quarry in the hill country, . . .

[6]And King Solomon and all the congregation of Israel, who had assembled before him, were before the ark, sacrificing so many sheep and oxen that they could not be counted or numbered.

[5]King Solomon offered as a sacrifice twenty-two thousand oxen and a hundred and twenty thousand sheep. . . . (1)

Solomon's Gilt

To one hundred fifty thousand men
The construction was entrusted
For twenty years, and in the end,
It was fully gold-encrusted.

The Temple had a cornerstone;
It, too, was gold-encrusted.
Since everything was made of gold,
The Temple never rusted.

With the Temple done, in gratitude,
There was a celebration:
Twenty thousand oxen barbecued,
Befitting the occasion.

And to insure there would be enough,
King Solomon was proffering
Another hundred thousand sheep
To the Lord as a burnt offering.

In a way, it seems ironical
That the Temple had been built
By the only king in Chronicles
Who didn't suffer for his gilt.

II Chronicles 12:16, 14:1, 26:23

[16]And Rehoboam slept with his fathers, . . .
[1]So Abijah slept with his fathers, . . .
[23]And Uzziah slept with his fathers, . . . (1)

Each King "Slept with His Fathers"

The second book of Chronicles
Is just that: a chronology
Of the Good Lord's list of monarchs
In His people's genealogy.

It starts out with King Solomon;
Zedekiah, last of all.
Solomon saw the Temple rise;
Zedekiah saw it fall.

It further states, in great detail,
Who sinned and who was hallowed,
And it tells which king preceded which
And names each king that followed.

In Chronicles, no king has died;
Instead, they use the phrase
Each king "slept with his fathers,"
Which you don't hear nowadays.

Still, the Good Book isn't sexist.
Just think of all the fuss
If a king "slept with his mother,"
As occurred with Oedipus.

Post-face

With that tender thought, we now say "adieu"
To this rather bizarre Bible study.
I'm sure you'll agree that it's funnier, too,
Than the original text — and less bloody.

Though innocent fun is this book's raison d'être,
It may be precisely what's needed
To focus attention on Scripture, I'll bet,
So dust off your Bible and read it!

About the Author

Born in 1915 in St. Louis, Missouri, Ben Milder is the author of more than 700 poems of light verse written over the past 35 years. In 1979, his book *The Fine Art of Prescribing Glasses Without Making a Spectacle of Yourself* won the American Medical Writers Association's Best New Book of the Year Award. Ben Milder's light verse has been published in many magazines and journals including the *Palm Beach Post*, *Milwaukee Sentinel*, the *St. Louis Post-Dispatch*, *The Critic*, *Long Island Night Life*, and in the anthology *The Best of Medical Humor*. Professor of Clinical Ophthalmology at Washington University School of Medicine, Dr. Milder resides in St. Louis with his wife, Jeanne.